The IEA Health and Welfare Unit

Choice in Welfare No. 11

Equal Opportunities:

A Feminist Fallacy

Michael Levin
Ellen Frankel Paul
David Conway
Ivy Papps
Joan Kennedy Taylor
Wendy McElroy

Edited by Caroline Quest

IEA Health and Welfare Unit
London, 1992

First published in 1992
by
The IEA Health and Welfare Unit
2 Lord North St
London SW1P 3LB

ISBN 0-255 36272-2

Typeset by the IEA Health and Welfare Unit
in New Century Schoolbook 11 on 12 point
Printed in Great Britain by
Goron Pro-Print Co. Ltd
Churchill Industrial Estate, Lancing, West Sussex

Contents

page

Foreword

It is increasingly taken for granted that if women make up 50 per cent of the population, then every occupation should also be 50 per cent female. If the proportion is lower than 50 per cent the conclusion is drawn that discrimination must have occurred, in which case the state can legitimately interpose some reverse discrimination to even up the score. This collection of essays, mostly written by women, provides a ringing challenge to the prevailing orthodoxy. Positive discrimination, say the authors, is not in the interests of either women or society at large and is not compatible with a society of free individuals, each contributing to the common good as they believe best. In such a society, work and other opportunities should be open to the talents, not apportioned according to a quota system.

The collection is also important for the contribution it makes to putting 'women's studies' on a more scholarly footing. A considerable proportion of feminist writing has taken the extreme form of analysing women as a class, not dissimilar from the Marxist proletariat. It is almost as if old Marxist tracts have been dusted off, typed onto a floppy disc and subjected to a computer 'search and replace' command: *search for:* 'proletariat', *replace with:* 'women'; *search for:* 'bourgeoisie', *replace with:* 'men'. With the rest of the Marxist volume left intact, the result is that men are now the ruling class and women the exploited class.

The consequence of regarding men as the ruling class is that their opinions on some matters, particularly the family, are not to be taken seriously. As exploiters of women, men should simply not be listened to. Not that this is an advantage to all women. Those females who do not subscribe to the correct feminist perspective are denounced as 'little women' suffering from false consciousness and can also be disregarded. Such arguments amount to a wholesale rejection of rational debate as a means of resolving differences of view. By contrast, the contributions to the present volume have challenged some of the high points of feminist orthodoxy in a quiet, scholarly manner.

I must, therefore, place on record my thanks to Caroline Quest for assembling a first class volume of essays, which I hope will soon be followed by another collection on the same theme.

David G. Green

The Authors

Professor Michael Levin teaches philosophy at the City College and Graduate Centre of the City University of New York. He is the author of *Metaphysics and the Mind-Body Problem* (1979) and *Feminism and Freedom* (1987). He has published extensively in the technical areas of philosophy, primarily philosophy of science and foundations of logic and mathematics. He has also written extensively about feminism, race relations, and equal opportunity.

Ellen Frankel Paul is Deputy Director of the Social Philosophy and Policy Centre and Professor of Political Science at Bowling Green State University. She received her doctorate from the Government Department at Harvard University in 1976. Professor Paul is the author of numerous scholarly articles, and the author or editor of 24 books, including *Moral Revolution and Economic Science* (1979), *Property Rights and Eminent Domain* (1987), and *Equity and Gender: The Comparable Worth Debate* (1989).

David Conway is Reader in Philosophy and Head of the School of Philosophy and Religious Studies at Middlesex Polytechnic. He was educated at Clare College, Cambridge, and University College, London. Dr Conway's publications include *A Farewell to Marx: An Outline and Appraisal of His Theories* (1987).

Ivy Papps is Senior Lecturer in Economics at the University of Durham. Her research has concentrated on the allocation of resources in situations where conventional monetised markets either do not exist or are not the primary means by which allocative decisions are made. Dr Papps has published widely in books and academic journals on the economics of the family, environmental economics and cost-benefit analysis. She is currently working on a book on the determinants of the socio-economic condition of women.

Joan Kennedy Taylor is the author of *Reclaiming the Mainstream: Individualist Feminism Rediscovered* (1992). She has directed book programmes for the Manhattan Institute and the Foundation for Economic Education; was an editor for *The Libertarian Review* and *The Freeman*; has written for US publications including *Reason, The Wall Street Journal,* and *Success* magazine; and contributed to the books *Freedom, Feminism, and the State* (1982) and *Beyond the Status Quo: Policy Proposals for America* (1985). She was a commentator on the Cato Institute syndicated radio programme, 'Byline', and is the National Co-ordinator of the US Association of Libertarian Feminists.

Wendy McElroy is a freelance writer and lecturer. She is the editor of *Freedom, Feminism and the State* (1982) and a frequent contributor to such periodicals as *The Journal of Libertarian Studies,* and *The Freeman*. She is Managing Editor of Knowledge Products.

Caroline Quest is currently Associate Editor at the IEA Health and Welfare Unit and Teaching/Research Fellow at the London Management Centre. She is co-author of *Competing for the Disabled* (1989) (with Charles B. Galasko) and has written on social policy issues. Educated in Israel and England she has degrees in social policy and business administration (MBA).

Editor's Introduction

Caroline Quest

Throughout every walk of public life from the Bar to the NHS, through schools, universities, charities, banks, newspapers, government departments, the police, and more—a growing number of disparate organisations stand united in transmitting to politicians and law-makers, students, teachers and ordinary people the feminist message about work. This is that the interests of both women and of justice are best served by ever more extensive interference with, and regulation of, the spontaneous workings of the free market. It is claimed by this coalition that such interference is necessary to ensure that women achieve a representation in the workplace no different from that of men, and it is further claimed that the current under-representation of women in top jobs is both inimical to their interests as well as a sign of their being victims of unjustifiable sex discrimination.

An indication of how successfully this message has been put across is the recent launch of the Prime Minister's own equal opportunity project, Opportunity 2000 and Charter for Women. These initiatives supplement the already extensive activities of the Equal Opportunities Commission which spent over a record £4.5 million last year promoting and enforcing sex equality. And the EC has characteristically been no less profligate in pursuing the same ends. The third community action programme 1991-95, 'Equal Opportunities for Women and Men', promises still more equalising legislation, equal opportunity programmes, and 'awareness-raising' initiatives.

Against this background, the present collection of essays stands out as one of the very few recent works offering an opposing point of view. The authors challenge the widely-held assumption that differences in the positions of men and women at work are the result of the absence of equal opportunities. Anti-discrimination and equal-pay laws are condemned as abrogations of freedom and private property. Such interventions into the free market do not enhance justice; they undermine it. They weaken the institutions of private property, freedom of contract, and equality before the law which form the foundations of a free society on which the prosperity of women and society at large depends. In their own way each of the authors illustrates this.

Most of the contributors are American. There are two likely reasons for this. First, the US has succumbed less to the temptations of socialist experiment. Consequently, market institutions have been subject to far less interference there than in the UK. This has made it easier for the Americans to see the movement for sex equality at work for the assault on market institutions that it really is. Second, this movement has gone further in the US than in the UK because it has been able to ride on the back of the powerful civil rights campaign of the 1960s.

The first author, Professor Michael Levin, calls into question the widely held belief that the occupancy by men of more of the top jobs in society than women implies that women are victims of unfair discrimination. Professor Levin argues that what accounts for the fact that more of the top jobs are filled by men is less the outcome of malign and unjust discrimination than it is the product of wholly innocuous genetically-based group differences in preference and ability. Women, he argues, are genetically predisposed to have other priorities than paid work. Their 'under-representation' in top positions is a result of innate sex differences and not coercion, hence there is no injustice.

By means of an extended case study, Professor Ellen Frankel Paul shows how current anti-discrimination laws have a highly damaging effect on two of the legal institutions upon which a free society is reliant: freedom of contract between employer and employee and the rule of law. The case study in question concerns a leading American battery manufacturer, Johnson

Controls, and their 1978 policy not to employ fertile women in jobs requiring exposure to lead which could harm any children they might conceive. In 1991, this policy was judged discriminatory by the US Supreme Court. The Court judged that Johnson Controls were discriminating against fertile women by not allowing them to decide for themselves whether to assume this risk. Professor Paul argues that this decision restricts the freedom employers have to make rational decisions, and undermines the rule of law by dispensing with consistent, predictable, and impartial laws. Because Johnson Controls can no longer avoid hiring fertile women it runs the risk of potential law-suits by women whose children are born damaged from exposure to lead.

David Conway argues that the biological differences between the sexes necessitates that it is mothers rather than fathers who look after their small children. Women are therefore, more likely than men to withdraw temporarily from full-time employment in the early stages of parenthood. This must make it more risky or costly for an employer to hire a women over an equally talented man, when they must be paid the same. Because equal opportunities legislation prevents employers from being able to respond rationally to these differences, the costs of production must be greater where it is in force to the detriment of both men and women. Given that the fundamental reason women engage in paid employment is to maximise household income, then women's interests are best served by a system in which employers are free to select whoever they judge best to employ for the job. According to Dr Conway the proper place for using the law to secure equity for women is in the family courts rather than the workplace, where it serves no one's interests but those who administer the legislation.

It is a basic assumption made by those favouring equal opportunities policies that the well-being of women can be improved by increasing their number in paid work. The EC for example, has this as one of its prime objectives. Against this assumption, Dr Ivy Papps argues that what matters so far as the well-being of an individual is concerned is the value to them of the resources at their disposal.

4

Women's well-being is therefore more accurately measured by their average wage level than by their number in paid employment. Governments wishing to intervene to improve the position of women might do better to support initiatives such as training that increase the demand for women's labour, and with it the wage they can command, rather than focusing on ways to enable more women to work.

Joan Kennedy Taylor examines the causes underlying the recent sudden increase in the numbers of single mothers who are on welfare and the emergence in Western cities of an underclass who prefer to secure their income by means of predation and violent crime than by work. She attributes both recent trends to the cumulative effect of misguided attempts by legislators to protect society's relatively disadvantaged against arbitrarily defined 'substandard' working and living conditions. This is achieved by imposing minimum permissible standards in these areas. The imposition of minimum standards has prevented the poorest women from being able to maintain themselves and their dependants independently through their own efforts, by engaging in cottage industries, taking boarders, and child-minding. The result has been to drive poor families into dependency on the welfare state. Taylor argues that the prospects of poor women are quite clearly best served by less rather than more state interference in the realm of employment.

Wendy McElroy questions whether preferential hiring policies are either just or in the best interests of women. McElroy points out that the women who benefit today from preferential hiring are not the victims of past discrimination against women. Nor are those who are called upon today to bear the costs—namely, the men passed over for selection on grounds of their sex—the culprits of past discrimination.

So far as the benefits to women of preferential policies are concerned, McElroy argues that the system of quotas to which these policies inexorably lead is liable to harm rather than benefit women on the whole. They would inflame resentment in men who had been passed over in favour of less-well qualified women. Such policies would stigmatise able women as inferior, by rendering it uncertain whether they owed any positions of prestige they enjoyed to personal merit or merely to their gender.

As to where the book leaves women and their role in the workplace and in their families, the best possible conditions for them are those which would spontaneously emerge in a free society. In such a society, women would automatically tend not to be discriminated against on grounds of sex alone. This is because, as the authors point out, a competitive labour market would not tolerate such economically inefficient ways of allocating labour.

In a free society, there would also be no need for a concern to secure 'equal pay' between men and women. This is because in a competitive market each person tends to receive that financial reward mutually accepted by employer and employee as appropriate for the given job at the given time. There is no absolute or 'right' measure of the appropriate reward. Jobs do not have an intrinsic value which can be measured. The value of work can only be calculated subjectively and therefore arbitrarily. Even the most sophisticated methods of job evaluation cannot change the fact that the worth of a job is simply that which employers and consumers are willing to pay for it. If women's average pay level was lower than that of men, this could be because women had chosen to distribute their energies in a manner different from men, or because they were on average less talented than men. Those women who wished to earn as much as men would have the opportunity to do so, provided they had the same level of commitment, skills and talents.

That women do have different priorities from men has emerged as a finding from recent studies undertaken on both sides of the Atlantic.[1] Because women necessarily take the central child care role they do not rate income as the most important aspect of their work. Commendably enough, women look for jobs with convenient hours and which are within easy travelling distance from home.[2]

As if anti-discrimination laws, equal opportunity programmes and equal pay legislation were not enough, the working women's lobby is now stepping up its demand for subsidised child care. This demand usually emphasises the increased choice subsidised child care would give to women. The Equal Opportunity Commission, for example, promotes state subsidised child care as *The*

Key to Real Choice.[3] But how can this be the case? State-funded child care cannot achieve a net gain in free choice, since those forced into paying for it lose their freedom to choose what to do with their income. And what are the grounds for the government favouring pre-school child care for women over say on-site gymnasiums for men? The benefits to society of improving the health of male workers may very well outweigh the benefits of enabling mothers of young children to work, and it seems almost certain to outweigh the emotional cost to babies of full-time institutional day care.[4]

Mothers cannot be the talented and valued employees day-care supporters claim. At least, not talented and valued enough for the majority of employers to find it worthwhile to arrange day care without subsidies. The fact that the majority of employers find day care unprofitable is because it is inefficient. Venture capital is sufficiently plentiful and employers and entrepreneurs sufficiently astute to have provided day care for the pre-school children of working mothers if it were profitable to do so.

In a free society, there would be no need of state subsidy for child care to enable women to go out to work. Either their ability alone would merit pay sufficient to cover the costs of child care without need of subsidy, or there would be no external economic imperative compelling them to go out to work. Where the *only* financial support upon which mothers of small children could rely was that of the fathers of the children, young women would think twice about risking having children. Similarly, young men would think twice about risking having children through casual sex, if they knew they would be legally compelled to maintain any that might result from these liaisons.

In a free society, therefore, the self-reliant two-parent family would be the normal institution within which children would be born and raised. Surely, this would be best for the children and for any woman who values the well-being of children as well as herself.

Notes

1 Richard Lynn, *The Secret of the Miracle Economy*, London: The Social Affairs Unit, 1991. For an overview of US research see George Gilder, 'The Myth of the Role Revolution', in Nicholas Davidson (ed.), *Gender Sanity: The Case Against Feminism*, New York: University Press of America, 1989, pp. 231-3.

2 Jean Martin and Ceridwen Roberts, *Women and Employment: A Lifetime Perspective*, London: HMSO, 1984.

3 London: HMSO, 1990.

4 William and Wendy Dreskin, 'Day care and Children', in *Gender Sanity, op. cit.*

1

Women, Work, Biology, Justice

Michael Levin

Feminism, Family and Justice

Despite a show of great internal diversity made by feminists
themselves, feminism is defined by one central, constant tenet:
the unfairness of sex roles.[1] It is not only that men and women
are expected to act differently, the charge runs; men do more and
occupy the positions of power. The sexes do not receive equal
pieces of the pie.

Feminists have pressed this charge with special vehemence
against 'traditional' family roles, and their hostility has been
influential. Praising parenthood is again acceptable, but suggesting that mothers have a special relation to their children is still
a gaffe. Motherhood is no longer called a plot to oppress women,
as it was during the vogue of conspiracy theories, such theories
having collapsed from internal incoherence. It makes no sense,
after all, to accuse the family of turning girls into appearance-
mad ninnies lacking useful skills, and capitalism of exploitat-
ively paying women less than their skills are worth. What has
survived of this accusation is the place of the family in fostering
'economic inequality'. Men outearn women, and dominate the top
ranks of organizations whose lower strata women manage to
penetrate, because women are confined by domestic duties. Child
care consumes much of a woman's energy and limits her
investment of what remains. Women gravitate to routine clerical
tasks, for instance, so they can leave and re-enter the workforce
without loss of earning power. A keyboard operator can quit to
raise children and find a similar job five years later; not so for a

Vice-President for Purchasing. Single women with uninterrupted work histories earn as much as men,[2] but the workforce participation of women with families displays costly discontinuities. The average sex difference in number of years spent with their current employer explains about four per cent of the male/female wage gap; other 'work experience' variables account for 11 per cent more, and the characteristics of jobs chosen by women—which, as noted, reflect female domestic burdens as well as female skills—explain most of the rest.[3] Conversely, female occupational attainment means deferred motherhood, less time spent with fewer children, or no marriage and children at all. Male attainment does not compromise fatherhood similarly. Of course, dad could also spend more time with the kids by staying home, but since he is the one expected to secure an income, little of his work time is deducted from family time.

It is this asymmetry that is deemed unfair. Why should it be the woman who stays home? Why, when both mother and father work, should it be the mother who also oversees domestic matters? And this asymmetry, if it is indeed unfair, creates a case for recompensing women and protecting their future claims by such measures as affirmative action, higher pay for female-dominated jobs, day care and workplace redesign. Yet no sex difference in economic behaviour, or anything else, is in itself unfair. It is not *unfair* that men are stronger than women, or that, as a consequence, men hit baseballs further. (And once it is recognised as no injustice, this fact of biology ceases to be seen as an evil of any sort.) That there is a long step from inequality to injustice is lost on many writers. Thus, having expounded the family-role theory of lower female earnings, Victor Fuchs[4] thereafter describes them as 'inequities' and 'a great economic toll taken from women [by] the demands of motherhood',[5] as if that is what he has shown them to be. But 'inequity' and 'toll' are normative notions implying *blame*. The assumption of domestic duties by females is blameworthy only if it *wrongfully* causes *bad* economic outcomes, a verdict not sustained by differences in outcome alone. Failure to be professional baseball players is not a *toll* taken on women by their smaller muscles. Some further argument is needed to establish 'inequity.'

To be sure, many feminists impatiently demand measures to increase female earning power on the ground that women *need* them. Unwed mothers and divorcees (re-)entering the workforce are apt to lack marketable skills, and an increasing number of married couples need (i.e. want) two incomes. But an appeal to needs, whatever its other merits,[6] simply changes the subject. For it no longer represents the economic position of women as inequitable or unfair—women's claim to more money is said to follow just from the alleged need of some women for more. The issue of justice has been abandoned.[7]

From Inequality to Inequity

The true path from inequality to inequity passes through the territory of 'unequal opportunity', limits imposed by one party on another in the pursuit of some significant good. Differences in strength and co-ordination don't rankle most egalitarians because they are natural, innocently caused. Systematic differences in wealth and power are suspect not merely because wealth and power matter more than physical strength, but because, most egalitarians assume, these differences would not have existed had opportunities been equal. This assumption rests in turn on the idea that everyone wants wealth and power equally intensely and is by nature equally able to get them. Given this assumption, even congenital group differences imply past mistreatment—of the ancestors of the congenitally less able group. What is wrong with inequality is how it is assumed to have come about. At any rate, if you ask an egalitarian what is *unfair* about inequalities in wealth and power, you will usually find his answer is some variant of 'no great fortune without a great crime'.

There are admittedly some egalitarians who recognize 'innocent' inequality, but want it annulled anyway. One subgroup takes it as an axiom that necessities like food should be available to all, whatever caused their present unequal distribution. This brand of egalitarianism does not concern us, however, since, as noted, needs-based claims are not claims of justice, and anyway moral axioms resist rational assessment.

Other egalitarians rely on an old argument, lately revived by Rawls,[8] to *prove* that natural ability should not benefit its possessor. Natural ability, distributed by a 'natural lottery' in genes and upbringing, is unchosen and not the result of effort; it is therefore undeserved; therefore its fruits are undeserved. But like the appeal to needs, this argument strays from the topic of justice. It has no bearing at all on compensatory justice, the restoration of wrongful loss. Nor does it concern distributive justice, unless the talent distributor is personified—as God, say—and criticized for favouritism. Certainly, if the differential effects of natural talent were wrongs done to the untalented, one would expect there to be someone whose duty it is to annul them, but it seems impossible to say who that someone is.

Lest these points appear to be quibbles over the word 'justice', it is useful to note why this influential argument is intrinsically unsound. In a nutshell, it conflates *entitlement* with *entitlement to title*, a distinction best explained by example. Suppose a (unnatural) lottery promises £1,000 to the holder of ticket number 77, and by luck I buy ticket number 77. I didn't deserve to buy that ticket, but, having bought it, I do deserve the £1,000. I have done something to deserve the money without doing anything to be the one who deserves it. Again: I own a gem I happen to notice in the ground, without having done anything to deserve to notice it. Again: while Newton didn't deserve to be born with the brains to invent calculus, he does deserve credit for inventing calculus, since he is the one who invented it. That is what 'deserves credit for inventing calculus' means, and is not to be confused with 'deserves credit for having been born with the brains needed for creditable brainwork'. The natural lottery argument is persuasive because there is no evident reason why some people should be smarter, better looking and more likeable than others. But this response to natural inequality begs the question. Without some initial presumption that people *should* be equally well endowed, there is nothing wrong with—hence nothing unjust about—the natural lottery. There may be no reason some people should be smarter, etc., than others, but also no reason they should not be, either.

In practice, feminists seldom invoke the natural lottery argument. For one thing it emphasises outcome differences produced by differences in ability, not differences in motivation.

Even Rawlsians see no injustice in lacking a supposed good out of lack of interest in getting it. Since sex differences in economic outcome owe at least as much to sex differences in motivation as ability, the argument gets no purchase. For another thing, egalitarians of all sorts are extremely reluctant to acknowledge even innocently caused race or sex differences. One will have to search a long time for a feminist boldly arguing that science is unfair to women because men are better at it. And when group differences are taboo, the natural lottery argument is out of reach.

Absent the natural lottery argument, the only quarrel there can reasonably be with group inequality is its cause. Egalitarians are thus stuck where we found them, faulting group differences for the denials of equal opportunity they supposedly reflect. Egalitarian verdicts thus rest, like legal verdicts, on a theory of fact, in this case a theory of the origin of group difference. Sexual egalitarianism in particular rests its charge of economic inequality on the theory that sex differences arose from a thwarting of the wills of women—a thwarting summarized as 'oppression' and 'discrimination' and 'sexism'. Conversely, if women earn less than men out of a clear-headed preference for other ends, there is no injustice.

Biology and Justice

The concession that family roles cause income disparities might be thought to settle the issue. Women earn less because they prefer to stay home. Feminists, however, simply dispute the 'prefer'. Females are 'conditioned' out of wanting prestige and power, they say, and into accepting conventional roles. Having learned to avoid conflict and self-assertion, women retreat into the home, conveniently freeing males of female competition. This conditioning is not considered a male plot—no explanation of it is given, in fact—but conspiracy theories are patently lurking in the background.

It is here that the biological innateness of sex differences becomes important. Biology shows that the preferences which generate sex roles are genetically determined, not learned. They are not the result of social manipulation. Arguably (see below) even learned preferences are consistent with free choice, as long as the learni[...]coerced. If so, female role choice may be free although me[...]d by 'conditioning', just as my pursuit of a promotion is free although mediated by a conditioned association between a promotion and more money. But biology short-circuits the need for such an argument, by showing that sex roles spontaneously express the basic human personality.

Feminists treat innate sex differentiation as if its main use, or misuse, was to prove the fitness of males to rule. This danger is imaginary (and probably perceived to be such by feminists). Not only are there no hordes of male chauvinist neo-Nazis waiting to bar women from law school on biological grounds, biology takes no stand whatever on questions of value. Biology *describes* men and women, and rating men better than women because men are more aggressive, or women better than men because women are more nurturant, makes as much biological sense as judging ducks better than horses because ducks quack. Ducks quack because quacking was adaptive when ducks evolved, just as sex differences have presumably been adaptive during human evolution. Biology does not rank the sexes, and makes no commitment about the ideal number of female physicists, the proper division of household chores, and other questions agitating gender moralists. To repeat: the significance of biology is juridical, not moral. Biology *exonerates* men (and 'society') by explaining male economic success in terms of innate, uncoerced differences in ability and desire. It provides a better theory of the behaviour of the sexes than does the oppression theory, thereby undercutting the claims of inequity supported by the oppression theory. Given innateness, women's assumption of domestic tasks and men's dominance in the work place are the aggregate effect of the sexes' different choices. It does not reflect thwarting. No one is to blame, because nothing blame-worthy was done. No steps are needed to alleviate the condition, because it is not a condition. Women are not owed compensation for systematic wrongs done to (other) women, since there were no such wrongs.

Difference Between the Sexes

That the sexes differ is scarcely disputed. As gauged by ordinary observation and psychometric tests, men are more aggressive, competitive, concerned with extra-familial status, and object-oriented than women: men excel at mathematics, visuo-spatial tasks, and abstraction. Women are more verbal, intuitively understanding of personal relations, and patient, better at routine algorithmic tasks; more apt to bond with their offspring. The question is the source of these differences, and three lines of evidence converge on its innateness.[9]

First, studies of fetal development confirm the hormonal differentiation of male and female brains in utero. Typically, the brains of all and only genetic males are exposed to and shaped by 'virilizing' androgens. In a number of 'natural experiments' involving the 'wrong' hormones, genetic females exposed to androgens have developed stereotypic male traits, and males insensitive to androgens have developed stereotypic female traits, in the face of social conditioning.

Second, there are known anatomical differences between the brains of men and women, notably in structures with which stereotypic behavioural differences are associated. For instance, the bridge between the right and left cerebral hemispheres is thicker in women, suggesting that female processing is less compartmentalized and therefore seemingly more 'intuitive'.

Third, sex differences are predicted by evolutionary theory. Fit genes are genes whose bodies reproduce them. So consider a gene with different contingency plans for finding itself housed in a male or female body. Since females can produce fewer half-copies of their genes than can males, a gene will instruct a female 'house' to be more selective about mates and to invest more energy in each of its (few) offspring. It will tell a male 'house' to try to impress those choosy females by displaying dominance over other males. (It will also make males more promiscuous and aroused by observable cues.) Such a gene will displace rival genes not encoding such plans. Speaking literally, mammalian strains whose females developed bonding mechanisms and whose males developed dominance-aggression were bound to succeed. *We*, the descendants of successful strains, are therefore likely to have such mechanisms.

Family Roles

It is easy to see how these differences would create economic and caretaker roles without discrimination or oppression. The new mother, more sensitive than her mate to infantile sounds, flooded with sex-specific hormones, bonds with her baby. Wanting, more than her mate, to be with and cosset her baby she stays with it. Her superior fine-motor co-ordination and tolerance for repetition further incline her to assume these tasks. Meanwhile her mate, preferring status and control of the physical environment, is out hunting mastodons or closing a deal. Resources are used most efficiently if the mother also assumes care of whatever counts as home. (Reinforcing these choices is the undoubted preference of young children for their mothers.) It is not that, absolutely speaking, women *like* domestic tasks and *dislike* competition, and vice-versa for men; women like domestic tasks *more than men do* while men like dominance *more than women do*, and this relative difference differentiates roles. Men outrank women in the hierarchical world of work because they seek higher positions more avidly. Nor do hierarchies favour men: they favour certain traits, such as objective thinking and ruthlessness. Women who 'think like men' do achieve hierarchical success; it is just that more men than women think like men. Wanting dominance more, men work harder for it and, other things being equal, achieve it more often. And other things are not equal, because of sex differences in abilities. Relatively technical, industrial societies such as ours tend to reward the highest levels of mathematical and analytical skills, where the male advantage is most pronounced. This is why the vast majority of scientific and engineering innovators have been, and may be expected to continue to be, men.

Income has a special meaning for men because it is an objective, public measure of status. By embodying the resources others are willing to exchange for a worker's efforts, his wages broadly conceived—salary, commissions, royalties—reflect his value in the eyes of others. This is a point not lost on professional athletes, who often demand minute pay increments to set them above rivals. Because of its symbolic dimension, money matters more to men than to women, so men work harder to get it. If men and women had precisely similar abilities, so that their efforts were equally valuable to others, men would still be expected to outearn women.

In short, even the most sophisticated family-role theories of economic behaviour tend to misdirect the causal arrows. The female assumption of domestic tasks does not cause male economic attainment; both phenomena are effects of an underlying cause, innate sex difference.

It is sometimes argued that women would fare better in a less hierarchical society. Perhaps, but it is hard to see how society could be less hierarchical. Social structures are inseparable from their constituent individuals; just as wolf packs exist because wolves band together, hierarchies exist because men make them, and will exist as long as men do. If extraterrestrial levellers one day eliminated every rank in every extant organization, men would simply create new rankings. Finally, it should be clear that the male competitiveness which creates hierarchies and facilitates male success within them does not *entitle* men to status or wealth, and need not for male attainment to be fair. Success flows from performance, not the readiness to perform. But because men try harder more often, they succeed more often in performing satisfactorily. Nobody is interfering with women, forcing them to the sidelines, when men expend energy on competition. Women prefer to do otherwise.

There is another way to put this point that should appeal to value relativists. The original rhetorical question, 'Why must it be women who stay home?' presumes that wage labour is a *good*, deprivation of which is harmful. But, barring some transcendental perspective, goodness is in the eye of the beholder. To say women desire extra-familial achievement less than men is to say that such achievement is not the good to women that it is to men. Its loss is therefore not the harm to women that it is to men. Human beings don't like to eat worms as much as robins do, so, barring some transcendental perspective from which the consumption of worms is an intrinsic good, oatmeal instead of worms for breakfast is not a *loss* humans incur because of their appetites.

Innate Sex Differences

Innate sex differences explain other aspects of the 'condition of working women' more successfully than oppression. Sex stereotypes themselves, for instance, are best understood as inductions from observed (innate) behaviour. People think boys are more competitive than girls because boys *are* more competitive. These stereotypic expectations reinforce innate differences when they turn into norms—when people start thinking girls *should* be daintier than boys—but biology is the motor of the whole process. People encourage girls to be dainty because daintiness is useful in activities which, as a matter of fact, most girls will elect. Still, stereotypes have their effect, and outcomes not mediated by stereotypes might seem fairer than the outcomes we do have. It might seem fairer if the proportion of women in science paralleled the raw distribution of scientific aptitudes, rather than this distribution plus the officiousness of parents discouraging their daughters' interest in science. However, since no one is forced to hold stereotypes, and the effects of stereotypes on their objects are also non-coercive, there is nothing wrong in the outcomes they mediate. Nobody forces a father to believe his son is more apt to become an engineer than his daughter, and nobody forces the daughter to be guided forever by her father's expectations. In any case, justice cannot really ask the father to ignore empirical observations when anticipating the life choices of his children. Such restraint is impossible anyway; people cannot help generalizing from experience. Men and women will behave as they do, and generalize as they do from their observations of each other's behaviour. Both are effects, differing only in remoteness, of our genes.

A second much-agonized-over phenomenon is the 'glass ceiling', the clustering of women at the bottom of hierarchies they do enter. This tendency is also explained if—holding other factors constant—first, degrees of competitiveness are distributed normally, second, mean male competitiveness exceeds female, and third, the variance for males slightly exceeds that for females. For example, let mean female competitiveness lie one male standard deviation, S_M, below the male mean, and let the female standard deviation be $0.8 \, S_M$. There will then be about four men for every woman at strata whose attainment requires average male competitiveness, but *25* men for every woman at strata requiring competitiveness $1 \, S_M$ above the male mean. Like trait distribution, the prevalence/rank curve is nonlinear.

A third phenomenon, just beginning to be recognised, is the financial near-futility of mothers working. Using US figures, assume a working mother grosses an impressive $35,000 annually. If her husband makes $45,000, her income is taxed at a net marginal rate of about 40 per cent, reducing it to $21,000. Retaining a baby-sitter at $5 an hour from say, 8.30 a.m. to 5.30 p.m. costs $11,250, more if the sitter assumes housekeeping duties. Group day care is cheaper, but never less than about $100 per child per week. Buying and maintaining a wardrobe of work clothing has been estimated[10] to cost $1,500 per year. Unwaged mothers also travel, but the net annual cost of commuting is at least $250. Working mothers must lunch at work and often lack the time or energy to cook family dinners; the net cost of food prepared by others in restaurants or 'take-away' establishments can be put conservatively at $1,000. So our working mother has netted at most $7,000, less given more pessimistic, and perhaps realistic, assumptions. What must be observed is that this erosion of income is due not to any defect in social policy, but the biological truism that children cannot care for themselves. Someone, whether it be their mother or her proxy, must care for them. As a proxy will not wish to spend her own resources on the children of others, the biological family will be asked to supply these resources in monetary form. Either way, the mother labours for her children—directly, by taking care of them, or indirectly, by transferring to her proxy the wages an employer has exchanged for her labour. Subsidized child care may sufficiently complicate this flow of resources to obscure its endpoints, but it will not 'liberate' women's productive energies (assuming they need liberating). Its main accomplishment, in fact, will be to force the childless to help raise the children of others. There are no free lunches, or free next generations.

A final biological truism is the pair-bonding of the sexes, which makes a man and a woman sharing resources the basic socio-economic unit. Since any reduction in a man's earning power thus harms some, namely his mate, affirmative action and 'comparable worth' are, in addition to being unwarranted by justice, necessarily self-defeating. Passing over Jim to hire Jane harms Jim's wife by as much as it helps Jane. The money supply being finite, Jane's salary can be raised to reflect 'comparable worth' only if Jim's salary is lowered, again depriving his wife. Helping one woman by harming another can hardly compensate women as a whole in any other way. Indeed, if Jane is married, Jane's *husband* gains what Jim's wife loses. (*Reductio ad absurdum*: Jim and Jane are married to each other, and every payday he ceremonially gives her part of his paycheque.) Even on their own terms—'improving the position of women'—affirmative action and comparable worth make sense only when advantaging unmarried women over bachelors. This is not widely realised because the sexes are conceived, like the races, as competing groups.

Confusions About Innateness

Appeal to innate sex differences prompts many objections and misunderstandings.

One is that sex roles must be learned because genes can't programme specific behaviour. 'There is no gene for changing nappies.' True, just as there is no gene for liking cookies—but did ever a child not like cookies? A taste for cookies *is* innate, not learned, cookie genes or no. More precisely, the taste of cookies is *unconditionally reinforcing*[11]—it is reinforcing, but not by association with other reinforcers. Children are born liking (i.e. being reinforced by) the taste of cookies; what they *learn* is where to find that taste—the contents of Crabtree and Evelyn tins, as it happens. Similarly, females do not like to produce smiles in babies because they associate the production of smiles in babies with other reinforcers, such as parental approval. Girls are innately disposed to like (i.e. to be reinforced by) evoking smiles from babies; what girls learn by association are methods for eliciting such responses. Different means are available in different environments. Around here, young women learn that babies can be made to smile by being diapered. In another culture they learn that babies smile when carried in a papoose. Changing nappies does, in fact, have a significant genetic component.[12]

Another problem is a felt conflict between genetic determination and free will. How can society be the result of biologically programmed choices, when behaviour resulting from programmed desires isn't *chosen*? What we don't have a say in is not free, and we don't have a say in our genes. In my cheerless world, puppets dance on strings of DNA tugged by evolution. Yet, however disquieting genetic causes may be in the abstract, we all unhesitatingly regard as free concrete everyday actions caused by innate desires. I eat lunch freely when I do so because I am hungry, as opposed to eating at gunpoint, despite not having had a say in whether my nervous system would transmit hunger pangs. Well, you may say, the hunger drive alone is innate; particular food preferences are learned (cookies aside), and therein lies our freedom. In fact, however, learned tastes are not acquired voluntarily either. You can decide to try caviar, but you cannot decide to like it. Food tastes are fully determined by genes plus environment. Yet even so, behaviour caused by those tastes—eating lunch when hungry—is usually regarded as free. Nobody regards himself as *forced* to select the sole over the turbot by his preference for sole. The upshot: freedom is doing what you want to do, wherever your wants came from. That being so, it is no oxymoron to speak of acting freely on genetically programmed wants.[13]

Not everyone accepts this resolution. Some thinkers, when they realise conditioned desires are no more voluntary than innate ones, do conclude that acting from desire is *never* free. Such thinkers regard as free only those actions, if there are any, that are not caused by desires at all. The self is thought to be free only when transcending the pressure of desire, perhaps by the use of 'reason', as separate from, indeed at odds with, its desires. Feminists veer toward such a view when they deplore the 'bondage' created by female interest in children, but the best-known advocate of such a view is Immanuel Kant. Kant's authority notwithstanding, though, the view is incoherent. How could its wants coerce the self, unless they made the self do what it did not *want* to do? Desires are fundamental constituents of the human personality; our desires can't push us around because there is no 'us' without them. The reason we have no say in which drives our genes give us is that there is no 'us' before the genes get to work. Our basic drives are neither freely chosen by us nor foisted on us; they *are* us.

A third confusion arises from the necessary role of the environment in mediating the expression of genes. All genes can do 'by themselves' is synthesize proteins, and even then the chemical environment must be propitious. No phenotypic trait is produced by genes alone; in particular, it is only in environments to which men and women have so far been exposed that human genotypes have produced phenotypically competitive males and nurturant females. Perhaps there are environments in which our genes would produce more similar males and females, whose market behaviour would in turn produce similar economic success. Don't we owe it to women to try to create such an environment, just as we owe it to children to try to create the most stimulating educational environment? Isn't this one of those cases in which we should use 'reason' to overcome nature?

Despite the immense volume of loose talk of this sort, there probably is no environment in which the major sex differences would fail to appear. The fittest genes prepare females to bond no matter what, for instance; it is hard to imagine a world in which maternal bonding is not adaptive, hence a world in which the 'bonding gene' expresses itself non-standardly. The emergence of bonding in every society so far certainly suggests that such a world, if it exists at all, is not humanly constructible. Furthermore, the institutions of a social order radically more unisex than ours might be so different as to preclude comparison of the positions of women here and there.

But let us assume that human intervention could create a world in which women are as successful economically as men. What needs most diligently to be noted is that failure to have created such a world to date is no part of the *cause* of women being 'poorer' than men. Nor will failure to create such a world in the future *prevent* women from being better off. Consequently, failure to create this world does not *deprive* women of anything, so no one is obliged to create this environment to restore to women what they have been deprived of. What somebody might have had is not what he now deserves, unless he has a prior right to be in that 'possible world'. I might have been better educated had a millionaire hired private tutors for me, but, when no millionaire volunteered, I was not *deprived* of tutoring.

Omissive causation is a moral, not a descriptive, category. My failure to educate my own children as well as possible is seen as causing their ignorance, because I am held to be obligated to educate them fully. Similarly, I was deprived of tutoring as a youth if some millionaire who was willing to help me, was dissuaded by threats from some enemy of mine. Here again, the possible situation was one I should have been in—i.e. one I wasn't in only because someone acted wrongly. So long, then, as no one has obstructed the development of environments in which women would have been as rich as men, it simply begs the question to argue that, if women could be as successful as men, their failure to be so is an injury. It must first be established that women should be as rich as men. Possibilities don't carry with them the right to be brought about.

Beyond Justice

Whether, absolutely speaking and aside from questions of justice, the economic expression of sex differences should be minimised, is an unanswerable question. The juridical perspective I have adopted cannot say what should or should not be done; it can only assess the reasons offered for action, and then only when these reasons are in some way connected to empirical data. Nonetheless, a few observations can be made about work and motherhood that remain within the orbit of fact.

When I said the next generation is not cost-free, I was assuming there will be a next generation. There need not be; women and men can decide not to have children, and a decline in fertility has indeed accompanied the entry of women into the workforce. The birthrate in the US has been below replacement since 1972. More important than this absolute decline in fertility has been a shift in who is reproducing. The birthrate has fallen most sharply among highly educated women, who are likeliest to see paid employment as an end in itself. This is also the female cohort of the highest average intelligence, which in the past bred the elites of succeeding generations. Meanwhile, the cohort reproducing most rapidly, the indigent on public assistance, represents society's least intelligent and orderly segment. A society undergoing such demographic change can hardly expect to remain technologically advanced, or to avoid a falling standard of living. No doubt the birthrate among the more educated and affluent is declining, in part, because attendant social changes make it difficult for them to raise their children in the manner they would prefer. In any case, everyone should be aware of the likely consequences of the female elite seeking employment, and everyone should think about ways to reverse the trends which discourage this cohort from reproducing.

A related issue is the effect on children of being raised by mother-proxies while their mothers work. In recent years a number of well-known authorities, including Jay Belsky, Penelope Leach and T. Berry Brazelton have expressed concern about the consignment of children under three years to day care. Such is the pressure to endorse wage labour for women that even these authorities go on to defend day care because of the presumed need for it. This is a *non sequitur*. The psychological effects of day care on children are what they are whether or not mothers need it. Philosophers have long warned of deducing 'oughts' from 'is's', but, as Wallace Matson has observed, the temptation nowadays is to deduce is's from oughts. It would be good if day care didn't harm children, so it doesn't. (Compare: it would be good if all the races had the same general intellectual ability, so they do.) Whether the effects of day care outweigh its value cannot be determined empirically, but the question of its effects must be considered independently, and cannot be answered simply in terms of its implications for working women.

There is an irony to be noted in the political Left's hearty endorsement of day care. The Left rejects the basic idea that preference-generated outcomes are fair, but this very suspicion of market forces might be expected to raise doubts about paid child care. After all, the idea that wage labour is alienating began on the Left. And surely it is in the case of raising children, if anywhere, that radical animadversions against profit make sense. A babysitter who sees her charge as a means to an income is more apt to 'commoditise' it than its mother, who cares for it from love. Yet the Left effuses over the dedicated professionals in day care centres who will raise children better than harried mothers. How the Left's concern with 'changing the role of women' has overwhelmed its displeasure with profit is a useful cautionary tale, of the difficulty of discussing 'justice for women' without fear of violating taboos.

Notes

1 See e.g. Janet Radcliff Richards, *The Sceptical Feminist*, Boston, Mass.: Routledge and Kegan Paul 1980, p. 5.

2 See Michael Levin, *Feminism and Freedom*, Rutgers, N.J.: Transaction, 1987, pp. 141f. and references.

3 June O'Neill, *The Determinants and Wage Effects of Occupational Segregation*, The Urban Institute: Washington, D.C., 1983, p. 69, table 25.

4 *Womens' Quest for Economic Equality*, Cambridge, Mass.: Harvard University Press, 1988, pp. 35-74.

5 See e.g. p. 150.

6 One might note the selective resignation of the argument. It takes utopian experiments to be feasible, while treating illegitimacy, divorce and the erosion of the middle class as givens.

7 Meeting needs may be a matter of justice if, as in Plato, 'justice' covers everything desirable in society. In its ordinary sense, and the sense assumed by the feminist critique, 'justice' is connected to malfeasance, compensation and equal treatment.

8 See John Rawls, *A Theory of Justice*, Cambridge, Mass.: Harvard University Press, 1988, index entry 'natural lottery'.

9 See *Feminism and Freedom*, chapter 3 for a survey of the literature with references, and chapters 4-5 for economic applications. An excellent, more up-to-date survey is Anne Moir and David Jessel, *Brain Sex*, N.Y.: Lyle Stuart, 1991.

10 Tamar Lewin, 'For Some Two-Paycheck Families, The Economics Don't Add Up', *New York Times*, April 21, 1991, p. 18.

11 i.e. It increases the probability of behaviour with which it is associated.

12 No doubt some specific nurturant behaviour is itself unlearned; females evidently find it unconditionally reinforcing to coo at babies.

13 The identification of freedom with doing what one wants is complicated by wants about wants. Is the smoker free who lights up because he wants to, but wishes he didn't want to? I ignore these problems here, since nobody is so conflict-ridden as to wish to want what the opposite sex does. Guilty homosexuals want to want what their own sex usually wants, but few heterosexuals wish to be homosexuals. For a discussion of brainwashing, compulsion and other puzzle cases, see *Feminism and Freedom*, pp. 28-9, and my *Metaphysics and the Mind-Body Problem*, Oxford: Oxford University Press, 1979, chapter 7.

2

Fetal Protection, Women's Rights, and Freedom of Contract

Ellen Frankel Paul

The term 'market economy' has become something of a buzzword for the 1990s. Communists, ex-Communists, their rebellious subjects and those no longer subject to their rule, media pundits, and even some academic experts in the West have embraced markets, urged privatization, while admitting the failure of central planning and socialism. This revolution of the *zeitgeist* is nothing less than remarkable, for a scant few years ago those few willing to embrace the free market were roundly and nearly universally condemned as throwbacks to the nineteenth century or worse. Yet, rejoicing on the part of capitalism's steadfast and long-suffering defenders may be a bit premature. One irony in this world-wide rediscovery of the value of individual freedom is that in the United States our Congress and courts continue to erode one of the linchpins of the free market: the principle of freedom of contract.

In a truly free market, those offering their services are free to negotiate with potential employers. Each worker will bring to the bargaining table skills, training, formal education, a work history, and personal characteristics. Each employer will require skills of a specified kind, years of prior experience or none, education suitable for the job, and will make other more subjective assessments of the suitability of a particular worker for employment. If a worker and an employer come to terms, one can assume mutual benefit from a bargain freely chosen by both sides.

The American labour market has not conformed to this 'ideal type' since the 1930s and the passage of the National Labour Relations Act 1935. This act enshrined in law the employer's obligation to bargain in good faith with a duly elected union and labelled as an 'unfair labour practice' any attempt by employers in their hiring practices to discourage union membership.[1] Thus, the freedom to contract of employers was limited by compelling them to negotiate with the representatives of unionised workers, while the freedom to contract of employees was also curtailed by barring them from negotiating terms of employment on their own. A series of further blows to the principle of freedom of contract have come more recently from anti-discrimination laws, and their effects on the market have been highly controversial, more insidious, and far less well understood than the effects of government-backed unionism.

The Civil Rights Act of 1964, which in its Title VII barred discrimination in employment on the basis of race, colour, religion, national origin, and sex, generated a host of progeny, including the Age Discrimination Act of 1967, the Pregnancy Discrimination Act of 1978, and the Americans with Disabilities Act of 1990. All of these pieces of legislation share several features in common: they skew the labour market to achieve social policies desired by legislators rather than those freely chosen by employers; they prevent employers from considering the additional costs involved in employing workers who fall into 'protected groups'; they subject all employment, promotion, and firing decisions affecting those favoured by a particular act to the prospect of litigation.

The Effects of Anti-discrimination Laws

With the creative assistance of judges, regulatory agencies, and presidential executive orders over the years, anti-discrimination laws have generated hundreds of thousands of charges of discrimination lodged with executive agencies and federal courts; encouraged state legislatures to emulate and expand their provisions; forced employers to engage in 'affirmative action' and hire by 'goals' that are nothing less than euphemisms for quotas in order to avoid liability; favoured certain workers (eg., minorities, women, and now the disabled) and handicapped others (primarily white males) in the competition for jobs; and, arguably, produced much social tension.[2] No longer, then, can one assume of any particular employment agreement that both parties to it have benefited because both have freely chosen to enter into it.

A meticulous analysis of the effects of anti-discrimination laws on the free market in the United States would be a mammoth undertaking. Therefore, this essay will confine itself to one issue arising from the anti-discrimination laws, an issue that illustrates particularly well the sorts of liberties that are lost when the terms of employment are interfered with *ex ante* by legislators and second-guessed *ex post* by judges. This issue is fetal protection policies: the attempt by some manufacturers who, unavoidably, use dangerous chemicals in their production processes to limit or prohibit the employment of fertile or pregnant women.[3] These policies have run squarely into anti-discrimination law, specifically Title VII of the Civil Rights Act of 1964 and its amendment by the Pregnancy Discrimination Act (PDA) of 1978.

A recent Supreme Court decision, *International Union, UAW v. Johnson Controls* (1991),[4] has galvanized vocal advocacy groups and focused public attention on fetal protection policies. Anti-discrimination suits turn on arcane issues of statutory interpretation, burdens of proof, judicially constructed theories and tests, and jesuitical readings of the precedents, and this case is no exception. All of this legal minutia usually serves to insulate these issues from public scrutiny and confine whatever debate there is to legal experts and their camp followers in the more refined media. However, the issue of fetal protection lends itself rather easily to exploitation, and the debate has played itself out on TV talk shows of the most sensationalist sort. Bedraggled business lobbyists have proved no match for representatives of women's groups or the American Civil Liberties Union (ACLU), accompanied by a working woman sterilized in order to retain her job. What has been lost in both the public hoop-la and the debate over legal niceties by judges and commentators, I shall argue, is a regard for the principle of freedom of contract and its vital role in a free market.

1. Fetal Protection Policies: The Social Background

During the past quarter-century, women in ever increasing numbers have entered the US workforce. No longer just secretaries, teachers, or nurses, they have invaded traditionally male preserves—police stations, firehouses, coal mines, and unionised, highly paid manufacturing jobs. This feminisation of the workforce is the result of many social forces and lifestyle changes, easily enumerated, but not easily quantifiable. Among these forces are changes in the law that made divorce easier and alimony less likely, and which forced many women, even those with young children, into becoming self-sufficient; twenty years of vicious inflation that made a middle-class family lifestyle virtually insupportable without two wage earners; the sexual revolution of the late-1960s and the women's rights movement that encouraged women to seek independence from men and to alter their dreams from the traditional marriage, children, and family to the executive suite; and anti-discrimination laws with their affirmative-action interpretations that encouraged women to enter non-traditional occupations and gave businesses an incentive (liability avoidance) to employ them.

The Pregnancy Discrimination Act

Two million working women become pregnant in the United States each year, which means that 71 per cent of pregnancies occur in working women. This makes pregnancy an important —and costly—management problem for businesses employing significant numbers of female workers. These management problems, however, have not been left exclusively to business to handle, for the Pregnancy Discrimination Act explicitly defined the Civil Rights Act's Title VII ban on employment discrimination on the basis of sex to include pregnancy. Many long-standing practices in the market-place were no longer permissible, such as firing a woman once her pregnancy became known, denying employment to a pregnant woman, or treating pregnant women differently from other employees who suffer temporary disabilities with respect to medical insurance, fringe benefits, or disability leave.

Thus, while Title VII itself mandated that employers ignore differences between men and women, as long as the women can fulfil the requirements of the job, the PDA went a step further by in effect demanding that employers likewise ignore pregnancy or treat it as they do all other (non-voluntary) disabilities. The PDA states that within Title VII:

> The terms 'because of sex' or 'on the basis of sex' include, but are not limited to, because of or on the basis of pregnancy, childbirth, or related medical conditions; and women affected by pregnancy, childbirth, or related medical conditions shall be treated the same for all employment-related purposes...as other persons not so affected *but similar in their ability or inability to work*.[5] (Emphasis added.)

One difference between men and women, however, that some employers found increasingly difficult to ignore is the heightened susceptibility of fetuses to dangerous chemicals in the workplace, fetuses that by nature—irrespective of law—only women can carry. Companies whose manufacturing processes could not eliminate the use of harmful chemicals or could not bring their use within safe limits for fetuses, responded with fetal protection policies, some more restrictive than others. Whether motivated by a moral regard for the welfare of future generations (as Johnson Controls contends) or out of a self-interested desire to avoid future tort liability for damaged offspring, or, even more insidiously,[6] to bar women from lucrative, male jobs (as Johnson's detractors argue), these policies did not sit well with female employees banned from their jobs or those denied employment, nor with women's advocacy and civil liberties groups.

Johnson Controls' policy, which triggered lawsuits in both federal and state courts,[7] was adopted in 1982. It replaced an earlier, more lenient policy put in place by the previous owner (Globe Union) of what would become, in 1978, Johnson's battery division. The production of batteries requires the use of lead, a chemical particularly harmful to young children and fetuses.[8] Johnson Controls after exploring its options decided that the previous policy, adopted by Globe Union in 1977, was no longer sufficient, in light of the additional scientific evidence that had emerged on the danger of lead exposure to fetuses. (Fetal exposure to lead could result in miscarriage, premature delivery, stillbirth, low birth weight, developmental problems, and other central nervous system disfunctions.) That policy included warning women of the dangers of lead exposure to fetuses, advising them that the company recommended that fertile women not work with lead if they were considering having children, and requiring that those still wishing to work with lead sign a statement acknowledging that they had been advised of the risks.

Johnson Controls concluded that despite its best efforts— expenditure of $15 million on lead-reduction technology since acquiring the battery division, its adherence to government approved safety limits for lead exposure for adults (set by the Occupational Safety and Health Administration (OSHA), the federal agency assigned the task of regulating safety standards in the workplace and monitoring compliance), and its insistence on showers, the use of respirators, and other safety devices for workers exposed to high levels of lead—a ban on the assignment of fertile women to high-exposure parts of the plant was necessary to protect their potential offspring.

The company was concerned, too, that under the previous policy eight women had given birth between 1979 and 1982 with excessive lead levels and that one of their children also had an excessive level. The 1982 policy bars women of childbearing capacity from being hired for high-exposure jobs or for jobs that would lead in the normal course of promotion to such jobs. Women already in such jobs were 'grandfathered in', that is, they were permitted to retain their jobs if their blood lead levels remained below 30 micrograms per decilitre (the level considered safe by OSHA for workers considering having families). Those transferred from such jobs retained their previous salaries, even if their new jobs were at lower wage rates. Women whose inability to bear children was medically documented could remain in high-exposure jobs or be hired for them. The company maintained that it was not its intention to force fertile women into being sterilized, although some women, including one of the plaintiffs who sued Johnson Controls, did claim that they were forced to choose between sterilization and loss of their jobs, and that they in fact chose sterilization. One plaintiff claimed, also, that her compensation was lowered upon removal from a high-lead exposure position to another.[9]

The Equal Employment Opportunity Commission

Johnson Controls is not unique in its adoption of fetal protection policies. The Equal Employment Opportunity Commission (EEOC, the agency charged under the Civil Rights Act with rule-making, arbitration of disputes, and lodging of lawsuits) cited a 1979 estimate that 100,000 jobs were at that time affected by such policies,[10] and another estimate much-quoted (by some of the judges who heard the appeals in *Johnson Controls*, the media, and commentators) put the number of jobs that might be affected in the future at between 15 and 20 million. Such prominent companies as B. F. Goodrich, General Motors Corp. Monsanto Co., and E. I. duPont de Nemours & Co. maintained similar policies.[11] The danger that such policies might spread to other industries, and that they might be extended beyond jobs exposing women to harmful chemicals to jobs requiring, perhaps, heavy lifting, is what prompted women's rights groups and the ACLU to view such policies as a danger to women's rights and opportunities almost on a par with restrictions on abortion. Isabelle Katz Pinzler, the ACLU's director of women's rights, argues that, 'Since time immemorial, the excuse for keeping women in their place has been because of their role in producing the next generation. The attitude of Johnson Controls is: "We know better than you. We can't allow women to make this decision. We have to make it for them"'.[12]

The public debate, both before and after the Supreme Court handed down its decision in *Johnson Controls*, has been framed in starkly contrasting images. On the women's rights side of the debate, as the quotation from Ms. Pinzler indicates, the issues are: a woman's right to decide what employment is best for her and for her actual and potential children, with the claim that she is in the best position to balance all factors, of health as well as economics; preserving the employment gains of women by fighting policies that would shrink their opportunities; opposing policies that force women to choose between destroying their fertility or losing their jobs; and fighting the reimposition of paternalistic policies, whether government enforced or adopted by individual companies. On management's side the pre-eminent issue (at least as posed for public consumption) is viewed as a moral one: protecting those who cannot choose for themselves, namely potential fetuses, from workplace hazards that might significantly impair them. In the words of Stanley S. Jaspan, Johnson Controls' lawyer before the Supreme Court, 'It violates common sense to require an employer to damage unborn children. A manufacturer that creates a hazard has an obligation to protect against injury for that hazard'.[13] The critics of fetal protection policies tend to view statements such as Mr. Jaspan's as cynical, as mere pretexts for reimposing the old-boy exclusivity on the plant floor.

2. Fetal Protection Policies—The Legal Quagmire

If we wish to see how an anti-discrimination statute can decimate freedom of contract, then *Johnson Controls* is exemplary. The tortured history of the case, as it wended its way from federal district court through two levels of appeal, first the Seventh Circuit and then the US Supreme Court, is also a nearly perfect example of how laws that seem fairly simple and straightforward to their framers can become twisted, distorted artifacts after years of exposure to creative counsel, judicial massaging, and unanticipated applications. Examining a fairly clear statute and a short amendment to it, the trial court judge and a majority of the judges on the Seventh Circuit found Johnson Controls' pleadings, replete with expert medical evidence, so compelling that they granted summary judgment *for the company*. The Supreme Court found the grant of summary judgment insupportable, the medical evidence debatable, and fetal protection policies on their face violative of anti-discrimination law. The lower courts embraced one paradigm of Title VII adjudication in reaching their conclusions, and the Supreme Court another.

The Rule of Law

My purpose, here, is not to examine this legal morass for its own sake, but rather as an illustration of the danger of interfering with the market-place in the name of civil rights. *Johnson Controls* bears close scrutiny not only for its effect on freedom of contract, but also for the damage it inflicts on another principle of critical importance to a free market and a free society. That principle is the rule of law, and one of its requirements is that individuals (or companies) not be held liable under one law for obeying the stipulations of another; this is a requirement that the Supreme Court likely transgressed by placing civil rights and tort liability on a collision course. Another component of the rule of law is that legal rules ought to be predictable in their application and readily comprehensible to those subject to them, features that the law as interpreted in *Johnson Controls* conspicuously lacks (a failure not unique by any means to antidiscrimination law).

Johnson Controls' initial victory was won in the United States District Court for the Eastern District of Wisconsin.[14] Chief Judge Warren framed the issue succinctly: 'whether a fetal protection policy which prohibits women who are capable of bearing children from working in jobs where there is a likelihood that their blood lead level will rise above 30 micrograms violates Title VII of the 1964 Civil Rights Act'.[15] After a review of the submissions of both parties and the law, he would conclude that it did not, and grant summary judgment to Johnson Controls.[16]

In reaching his decision, the chief judge conceded that fetal protection policies do not fit neatly into the usual two paradigms applied to Title VII cases by the courts, a problem recognized by other judges who have wrestled with the few similar cases.[17] In order to make such cases come out the way the judges desire, they have had to be creative with the two Title VII paradigms, bending here, snipping there, cobbling together a rationale that will reach the right end, even if doctrinally very messy. A brief overview of how judges have treated charges of, primarily, racial and sexual discrimination under Title VII will be necessary in order to see just how creative judges have been in dealing with challenges to fetal protection policies. Title VII reads in relevant part:

> It shall be an unlawful employment practice for an employer— (1) to fail or refuse to hire or discharge any individual, or otherwise to discriminate against any individual with respect to his compensation, terms, conditions, or privileges of employment, because of such individual's race, color, religion, sex, or national origin; or (2) to limit, segregate, or classify his employees or applicants for employment in any way which would deprive or tend to deprive any individual of employment opportunities or otherwise adversely affect his status as an employee, because of such individual's race, color, religion, sex, or national origin.[18]

Disparate Treatment and Disparate Impact

As Title VII cases progressed in the courts during the 1970s, judges articulated two paradigms for analyzing them—*disparate treatment* and *disparate impact*—both ultimately endorsed by the Supreme Court. *Disparate treatment* is intimately linked to the language of Title VII. One sort of problem that it addresses is facially discriminatory employment policies, that is, policies that merely in the stating of them violate some provision of Title VII. Employers can defend such policies only by showing that they fall within a narrow exception permitted under Title VII which has come to be known by an acronym: *BFOQ*. Discrimination is permissible 'in those certain instances where religion, sex, or national origin is a *bona fide occupational qualification* reasonably related to the normal operation of that particular business or enterprise'.[19] A BFOQ is a difficult defense to successfully mount, because the Supreme Court has read it narrowly to restrict it to job-related skills.

Given the difficulty of mounting a successful defense of fetal protection policies if an employer can only defend them as a BFOQ, and given many judges' inclination to uphold such policies as reasonable and socially justifiable in the interest of protecting the welfare of future generations, it is no wonder that judges have sought to squeeze these cases into the contours of a more appealing paradigm. A *disparate impact* theory of Title VII, the only other paradigm available, has had to serve those judges eager to uphold fetal protection, even though the fit is an uneasy one.

Disparate impact is a wholly created judicial artifact. It is aimed at facially neutral policies that work to the detriment of protected groups, policies 'fair in form, but discriminatory in operation'.[20] Policies successfully challenged under the disparate impact theory have included various objective hiring tools such as standardised intelligence tests, height and weight standards, and educational-attainment requirements.

Unlike disparate treatment cases, in which *intentional* discrimination must be proven (as Title VII explicitly requires), disparate impact requires no showing of intentional discrimination. Plaintiffs usually build their cases under this theory by showing evidence of statistical disparities between the employer's workforce (or a part of it) and the available minority or female workers in the area (or qualified minority or female workers in the area), and they must point to a particular employment practice—seemingly neutral—that works an unintentionally discriminatory effect. Employers can defend their policies by arguing *business necessity*, a somewhat broader category than disparate treatment's defense of BFOQ, thus an easier defense for businesses to make. Plaintiffs must then prove that this defense is spurious, and even if they cannot, they can still prevail if they can show that a policy with a less onerous effect on minorities or women would also serve the employer's legitimate business interest.

Fitting fetal protection policies on the Procrustean bed of disparate impact theory is no simple task. It requires considerable ingenuity, for the judge must argue that a policy that explicitly only applies to females is a facially neutral policy when it practically screams out that it is not. Acknowledging that the policy is explicitly discriminatory would drive it back under the inhospitable umbrella of disparate treatment from which it could not emerge unscathed, as the Supreme Court would eventually and definitively establish. Both Judge Warren and the majority of the Seventh Circuit Court of Appeals laboured valiantly to twist Johnson Controls' fetal protection policy into a facially neutral one with a disparate impact, and then to argue that business necessity justified its adoption. Their labours do not make a pretty picture (although for good measure, the Seventh Circuit majority did argue that even if they had considered the policy under the disparate treatment theory it would still pass muster as a bona fide occupational qualification). It is difficult to reproduce their argument for the neutrality of this seemingly non-neutral policy, since it was so blatantly contrived to reach the desired outcome, but what they seemed to be saying is that Johnson Controls was genuinely concerned with protecting fetal health, and that their concern led them to articulate a policy that affected only women because only women can carry fetuses.

It is fair to say that their reasoning was outcome driven. They found the medical evidence of potential fetal damage from lead exposure compelling and the medical evidence of damage to male reproductive capacity from lead exposure scant and confined to a few animal studies. Because lead stays in the blood, tissues, and bones for long periods after maternal exposure any alternative policy to protect fetuses was considered unlikely to achieve that objective. They were convinced that Johnson Controls' policy was reasonable and should be upheld. Therefore, they massaged the niceties of standard Title VII interpretation to secure this outcome.

Dissenting Views

Three dissents were lodged by four judges of the Seventh Circuit, two of them quite forceful, and somewhat curiously, penned by staunch conservatives, former professors at the University of Chicago Law School, and Reagan appointees to the court. They found the majority's manipulation of Title VII paradigms unacceptable, with one, Judge Posner, arguing that the case should have gone to trial and that the appropriate paradigm was disparate treatment and that the company should have had to defend itself under the BFOQ.

Judge Easterbrook, taking an even harder line and adhering to strict statutory interpretation, saw Johnson Controls' policy as 'sex discrimination, forbidden unless sex is a "bona fide occupational qualification"—which it is not'.[21] He was much concerned that the fetal protection policy treated an 'employee not as an individual but as a woman',[22] and that if such policies were judicially condoned more companies would adopt them and 20 million jobs might be lost to women. Indeed, the threat that such policies held of consigning women to low-paying 'women's work' led him to declare that this case 'is likely the most important sex-discrimination case in any court since 1964, when Congress enacted Title VII'.[23] Because such a policy assumes 'that women are less able than men to make decisions', and since pre-natal injuries had not occurred at Johnson Controls' battery operations, the policy could not be justified as a BFOQ, for such a defense can only be established when 'all or substantially all women would be unable to perform safely and efficiently the duties of the job'.[24] It is mere 'word play,' he argued, 'to say that "the job" at Johnson is to make batteries without risk to fetuses...'.[25] The possibility of tort liability, although not raised on appeal by the company, Judge Easterbrook considered and also found wanting, since Title VII bars employers from considering the additional costs involved in employing female workers.[26] 'Title VII', he emphasized, 'applies even when—*especially* when—discrimination is rational as the employer sees things'.[27] Defining tolerable risks and promulgating standards to protect future generations is, he thinks, properly the job of Congress or OSHA, and not of an individual company bent on enforcing on women exclusively, zero risk. Women should, as men, be entitled to consider their net risks when deciding to take higher paying jobs with medical and other benefits that would expose them or their fetuses to dangerous chemicals, rather than lower paying jobs with the attendant risks of no pre-natal care and no medical benefits.

When *Johnson Controls* reached the Supreme Court, Judge Easterbrook's arguments proved more persuasive than those of the Seventh Circuit's majority. With all justices concurring in the judgment of reversal,[28] the Court held that Title VII as amended by the Pregnancy Discrimination Act precludes sex-specific fetal protection policies. Judge Blackmun, delivering the Court's opinion, found obvious bias in Johnson Controls' policy; men, but not women, were given a choice about whether they wished to risk their reproductive health for a job exposing them to high levels of lead, and thus the policy 'explicitly discriminates

40

against women on the basis of their sex...[and] creates a facial classification based on gender'.[29] Thus, the Court rejected the lower court's selection of the disparate impact paradigm, finding that the policy fell squarely within disparate treatment analysis, but even here rejecting the appeals court's assertion that the policy could be justified as a BFOQ as well as the looser standard of disparate impact's business necessity. Reading the BFOQ narrowly, as the Court had in the past, Justice Blackmun pointed out that in order to qualify as a BFOQ a policy would have to relate to the 'essence' of the job, that is, to the 'central mission of the employer's business'.[30] Concern for future children, however, is not an 'essential aspect of battery-making',[31] because a woman's potential to bear children does not interfere with her ability to perform the job. Since the Pregnancy Discrimination Act's standard precludes discrimination against pregnant women unless they differ in their 'ability or inability to work', the Court concluded that Johnson Controls could not discriminate against potentially pregnant women unless this reproductive potential interfered with their performance of the job, which nothing in the record showed that it did. Therefore, Justice Blackmun had 'no difficulty in concluding that Johnson Controls cannot establish a BFOQ'.[32] His opinion ended with these words, emphasizing the importance to the Court of a woman's right to choose:

> It is no more appropriate for the courts than it is for individual employers to decide whether a woman's reproductive role is more important to herself and her family than her economic role. Congress has left this choice to the woman as hers to make.[33]

Employer Liability

Before reaching this ringing declaration of women's rights, Justice Blackmun did respond to the tort liability issue that concerned Judge Posner of the Seventh Circuit and Supreme Court Justices White, Rehnquist, and Kennedy in their concurring opinion, even though the issue was not before the Court. He concluded that without negligence, a court would have great difficulty in finding an employer liable for damage to a newborn. If Title VII bans fetal protection policies, as the Court now held that it did, and the employer informs the woman of all risks, and the employer had not acted negligently, 'the basis for holding an employer liable seems remote at best'.[34] Justice White and his two sympathizers did find this tort liability issue more troubling, worrying that adherence to Title VII might not insulate employers in tort suits against them in state courts.[35] Justice White is far less certain than Justice Blackmun that state courts will not be hospitable to claims of pre-natal damage. He states the following reasons for his concern: (1) that compliance with Title VII might not insulate defendants from tort liability in state courts; (2) warnings may preclude claims by injured employees, but women cannot waive the claims of their children; (3) it will be difficult for employers to know beforehand what will constitute negligence, because even compliance with OSHA standards has been held not to preclude state tort or criminal liability; (4) and as an additional worry, employers may be held *strictly liable* (a standard much more deleterious to defendants than the negligence standard) if their manufacturing process is considered 'abnormally dangerous'.

As we emerge from the legal quagmire, several essential arguments need to be kept in mind. The judges and justices who found fetal protection policies illegal under Title VII and the PDA placed great emphasis upon issues of women's autonomy, women's equal right with men to freedom of choice in employment, and their equal capacity to weigh benefits and costs of particularly dangerous jobs. They also found unpersuasive arguments of additional costs of employing women in jobs that exposed them to dangerous chemicals, particularly the speculative cost of future tort liability to prenatally injured offspring. Of great concern to them, in addition, was the spectre of similar fetal protection policies spreading to other sorts of jobs, with Justice Easterbrook even raising the spectre of prohibitions against female taxi drivers for fear of the noxious fumes or accidents to which their fetuses might be exposed.

3. Fetal Protection, Anti-discrimination, and a Free Economy

As I observed at the outset, my principal concern is not with the legal pyrotechnics, but rather with the implications of anti-discrimination laws to a free market and a free society. With this larger objective in mind, I do want to offer a few remarks in passing on the legal tergiversations experienced by Johnson Controls as its fetal protection policy traversed the court system.

Despite the lower courts' determination to view fetal protection within the disparate impact model, which at least held out the possibility that the policy could pass muster, it seems fairly clear that the Supreme Court's insistence that the policy is discriminatory on its face is more in harmony with Title VII precedents. But having said this, it is also fairly obvious why many judges found the disparate treatment paradigm unappealing. If there is a real danger of fetal harm from maternal exposure to lead in the workplace, and if lead lingers in the body for an appreciable period of time, and if batteries can only be produced with lead as a component—all hypotheses borne out by a preponderance of the expert testimony—then it is no wonder that judges wished to give Johnson Controls the leeway to protect fetuses, simply because it seemed reasonable to them to do so.

That Title VII, as judicially interpreted for the last twenty years, leads logically to the rejection of fetal protection policies says something very revealing about Title VII. If the additional costs of employing women cannot be considered by employers even when it appears rational for them to consider such costs, then Title VII requires companies not to be rational calculators, to systematically ignore a whole category of costs in making economic calculations. As Judge Easterbrook pointed out, it is in precisely those instances in which discrimination is rational that the anti-discrimination law acts to forbid employers from taking such costs into account. With the Supreme Court's decision in *Johnson Controls*, companies cannot ban fertile women from exposure to hazardous chemicals in the workplace, and as Justice White observed in his concurrence,[36] it is possible that with this ruling companies may not be able to prevent even pregnant women from engaging in such work.

Tort Liability, Conflicts of Law, and the Rule of Law

One of the more puzzling implications of the Supreme Court's decision in *Johnson Controls* is that companies, in complying with a ban on fetal protection policies, will be opening themselves to potential tort liability in state courts for children prenatally exposed to dangerous chemicals and suffering lifelong impairments because of such exposure. Companies, under the Supreme Court's reading of Title VII, cannot take such potential costs into account. But turning a blind eye to such potential liability forces companies into systematic miscalculations about their costs of production. Even more fundamentally, the Court has, rather cavalierly, placed employers in a Catch-22 situation where they are damned by the anti-discrimination law if they restrict fertile women from jobs that expose them to hazardous chemicals, or possibly damned by the tort law if they do permit women to work around dangerous substances and their fetuses are harmed.

While the Court dismissed the likelihood of successful tort cases brought by impaired offspring, to do so they had to dismiss over three decades of liability law expanded by judges eager to compensate even negligent victims at the expense of 'deep pocket' defendants. As Justice White adumbrated,[37] to dismiss such a possibility, as the majority did, is to ignore the shift from a negligence standard to a strict-liability standard, and further, to expose employers to unknown and, therefore, incalculable risks of exposure to liability even when the standard remains negligence but with its precise contours unknown. If adherence to Title VII will not insulate an employer from state tort liability, nor will a good faith adherence to OSHA's standards for workplace exposure to hazardous substances —both hypotheses that seem plausible, as Justice White observed—then the Court, by insisting that employers ignore such considerations in their employment policies, has thereby forced employers to act irresponsibly and, indeed, irrationally.

One wonders how to account for the Supreme Court's blithe dismissal of the liability issue. Can it be attributed to ignorance of the expansion of tort liability or, rather, to a hope that by expressing their belief that such suits would be unwinable that they would send a message to state court judges that they ought not look sympathetically upon such suits when they arise? The first alternative seems implausible, since the expansion of tort liability has become a highly controversial political issue. Several states have already legislated limits on punitive damages, and similar legislation has been proposed on the federal level. The defendants' bar and many commentators have condemned the expansion of strict liability, joint and several liability, and the explosion of punitive damage awards. The justices could not have been oblivious to all of this. The second explanation seems more likely: that by stating the wish it will become a reality. However, a third possibility does suggest itself—that the justices acted out of a cynical disregard for the likely effects of their decision, certainly a possibility too repugnant to contemplate.

Regardless of how one interprets the justices' casual dismissal of the liability issue, it is all too likely that juries when confronted with a brain-damaged, mentally and physically impaired youngster will be eager to reach down into a 'deep pocket'. Appeals courts may trim the punitive damage awards, but may also expand the traditional concepts of liability even further to allow for recovery. That is the history of tort liability, and companies that ignore such potentially staggering costs do so at their peril. But ignoring such costs is precisely what the Supreme Court mandated that companies do; that is the lesson of *Johnson Controls*.

A free market depends upon a basic structure of law. Without consistency, predictability, and impartiality in the law—all components of the concept of the 'rule of law'—a market system would be precarious, indeed. *Johnson Controls* threatens all three of these constituents of the rule of law. Consistency precludes conflicts of law, but that is precisely what adherence to Title VII may trigger, in the form of tort liability; predictability requires that one know in advance what sorts of actions will trigger liability, but the Court merely hopes that companies will not be exposed to liability for adherence to the anti-discrimination law; and finally, impartiality implies that all parties must be treated equally before the law, but *Johnson Controls'* implication is that some people are more equal than others and can thrust the costs of their imprudence on a 'deep pocket' corporate defendant.

Equal Rights and Freedom of Contract

A free-market system depends, most directly, on freedom of contract: on voluntary bargains between individuals who both benefit from the transaction. But anti-discrimination laws of the type that we have just examined make some traders more equal than others, and they do so in an Orwellian quest to secure equality for all. What Title VII demands is that employers hire women (and members of other so-called 'protected groups') whom as rational calculators they would not voluntarily hire. It requires that employers ignore any additional costs that hiring women may involve, and by dint of the Equal Pay Act of 1963 that they pay women and men the same wages for doing essentially the same jobs. To further remove the labour bargain from the ideal of a voluntary exchange, the Pregnancy Discrimination Act commands that employers in addition ignore the actual or potential pregnancy of women applicants and employees. Thus, by government fiat the terms of trade have been altered, and whole categories of perfectly rational business considerations rendered illegal. No longer can one assume that an offer of employment is freely entered into by an employer, because the employer has a gun to his head, and that gun is the threat of an EEOC filing or a discrimination lawsuit.

To make matters even worse, Title VII has not been interpreted as a protection for *all* employees, as its neutral language would imply and as Judge Easterbrook kept insisting,[38] but rather as in effect a results-orientated calculation of whether or not an accused employer has hired the right mix of 'protected' workers, i.e., blacks, Hispanics, American Indians, women, Eskimos, Aleuts, etc. That is the whole point of the typical disparate impact case: to demonstrate that a firm failed to employ the right percentage of blacks or women in comparison to their availability in the geographic area, or their proportion of the applicants or potential applicants.

'Equality' by Government fiat

Thus, in order to insulate themselves from discrimination charges and suits, employers must act irrationally, from the perspective of a strictly rational actor. And since the labour market can no longer be considered a free, voluntary market, one can never know after a bargain has been struck whether it is advantageous to both parties. Women, and other 'protected' workers will reap unearned rewards—or as the economists like to call them 'rents'—as beneficiaries of government coercion. Rather than achieving equal rights for all—the self-professed objective of anti-discrimination laws—some workers are made more equal than others, while all employers are forced to trade on terms that they may or may not have agreed to had their trades been left voluntary.

As a further illustration of how the search for equality by government fiat can take on ever more bizarre twists, it is worth perusing Mary E. Becker's 'From *Muller v. Oregon* to Fetal Vulnerability Policies', an influential law review article.[39] Becker deplores the Supreme Court's former paternalistic attitude towards women as expressed in their opinions from the early decades of this century. In cases such as *Muller v. Oregon* (1908),[40] the 'Old Court', roundly condemned in our era for its tenderness towards laissez-faire and freedom of contract, nevertheless upheld restrictive labour legislation when it affected women (and children, too). The Court allowed such interventions in the market-place out of a desire to 'protect' the weaker sex and insure healthy offspring. *Muller* upheld a ten-hour limitation on the number of hours that women could work each day, while in another case the Court approved a minimum wage for women, all practices declared violations of freedom of contract (under due process clauses of the US Constitution) when applied by legislatures to men. Becker deplores such legislation and the Court decisions that upheld them as paternalistic, and she views fetal protection policies as embracing the same kind of paternalistic attitude towards women, an attitude that implies that women are not capable of making decisions for themselves, and has the effect of limiting women's opportunities to compete with men for the most lucrative jobs. If ever fetal protection policies are necessary, and she seriously doubts that they would be, Becker prefers that regulation should come from Congress rather than from employers.

Becker's enthusiasm for congressional or executive-agency regulation over policies set by employers—who presumably would know their own industries better than regulators—ought to be considered anachronistic at this late date. Yet, her seeming obliviousness to the lessons of the public choice literature is not the most noteworthy aspect of her argument. What is truly remarkable about her position is her contention that if Congress sees fit to regulate for fetal protection, Becker wants women to be compensated for their exclusion. Either through affirmative action programs or through some scheme of more direct compensation, she wants to transfer the costs of natural differences between men and women onto employers and society. What could possibly justify this redistribution? Doesn't this smack of a paternalism similar to that which inspired the Old Court's willingness to accept restrictions on the hours of women's labour? How can Becker condemn the old sort of paternalism, and then recommend that women be given special benefits to compensate them for natural differences? Just because women are different from men by nature, why should feminists encourage them to seek handouts from male legislators? Isn't a demand for compensation nothing more than a new form of paternalism? Doesn't such a demand imply that women cannot compete in a free market? If women are at a competitive disadvantage as a result of biological differences, shouldn't their brief be against God or Nature, rather than employers who simply make rational calculations based on the way things actually are?

Becker's call for compensation for fetal protection represents a *reductio ad absurdum* of Title VII's and the PDA's insistence that members of some groups be made more equal than others in the name of achieving equality. A free-market system grounded on freedom of contract has these advantages over a governmentally enforced anti-discrimination regime: all transactions are voluntary; no one comes to the employment market-place with a government-guaranteed right to make the other party disregard rational, business calculations or face a lawsuit; trades, as a result, are mutually beneficial.

Conclusion

Fetal protection policies, now declared violative of the anti-discrimination law by the United States' most authoritative court, are just one illustration of the sort of behaviour that is perfectly acceptable in a free-market system. Anti-discrimination laws, however, by their very nature render many sorts of voluntary behaviour illegal. Principles that underpin a free economy

48

and a free society—such as freedom of contract and the rule of law—are undermined. A free-market system and anti-discrimination laws are on a collision course, and as time progresses and new wrinkles are added to these laws, freedom is sacrificed as government becomes a partner to nearly every employment decision, empowering one party and blindfolding the other.

A new sort of paternalism is replacing the old: judges declare in effect that women's rights matter, but not employers', that women's autonomy and women's freedom of choice matter, but not employers'. The new paternalism, in a twist on the old, wants women to be equal to men in the *results* of the employment process, and to achieve this *equality of results* it insists that employers ignore differences between men and women, differences that any rational business would consider. The old paternalists thought that they were protecting women from exploitation in the market-place, not that they were handicapping women in competing for the best jobs, as we now in our more enlightened age view the results of their efforts.[41] The new paternalists think that they are empowering women and treating them as equals, but in an even more enlightened age, will this attitude be seen as the logical outgrowth of the old paternalism, sharing with it the same premise—that women are a special class who cannot be left to fend for themselves in a free market? Such a more enlightened age might leave all people—men and women, blacks and whites—free to reach their own deals without Leviathan throwing its weight on one side of the bargaining table.

Notes

1 Subsequent legislation, the Taft-Hartley Act (1947), permitted states to enact so-called right-to-work legislation which precluded compulsory 'closed shops' and allowed workers who did not join the union at a company to still be employed there. Most of the states that have exercised this option have been southern states.

2 Of course, other observers might argue that the net social benefits of increased employment opportunities for members of groups previously discriminated against have outweighed whatever harm these acts have caused. To settle this difference of opinion by a utilitarian weighing of costs and benefits seems impossible, for there are simply too many millions of individual factors to be weighed in the scales, to say nothing of the problem of interpersonal comparisons of utility. But what is apparent, all utilitarian considerations to one side, is that these anti-discrimination laws have limited both the employers' and the employees' freedom to contract.

3 Other industries in which fetal protection policies have been introduced include petrochemicals, electronics, and hospitals. No accurate studies of the prevalence of such policies have been made, according to Joan E. Bertin, a lawyer for the American Civil Liberties Union (as quoted in 'High Court to Review Plans on Fertile Women at Work', *New York Times*, March 27, 1990).

4 111 S. Ct. 1196 (1991).

5 Pregnancy Discrimination Act of 1978, 42 U.S.C. § 2000e(k).

6 A point conceded by Johnson Controls' spokesmen in comments to the media. John P. Kennedy, general counsel for Johnson Controls, stated that the company was concerned with third-party lawsuits from neurologically damaged children exposed to lead in the womb. 'That's a legal liability a mother cannot waive', he is quoted as saying. 'Fetal Protection Policies Spark Intense Feelings from Women', *The Blade*, October 7, 1990. A similar statement was made by an unnamed company spokesman who said that the company was concerned about stockholder financial exposure to such suits. 'Who Decides Who Works at Jobs Imperiling Fetuses?', *New York Times*, September 2, 1990.

7 Johnson Controls' fetal protection policy did not fare well in a state court. A woman denied employment in one of its battery manufacturing plants in California challenged her denial as an act of sex discrimination under California's Fair Employment and Housing Act. The state appeals court considered a refusal to hire on the basis of a future possibility of pregnancy to be gender-based discrimination. *Johnson Controls v. California Fair Employment and Housing Commission*, Calif Ct App 4th Dist, No. G007029, 2/28/90.

8 In fact, since 1978 the use of lead paints in homes has been banned in the US and there is pressure in Congress today to go even further than this and mandate that all houses built before that date be inspected on resale and that warnings be provided to buyers. There is abundant evidence, and scientific agreement, on the harmfulness of lead to young children who might ingest large quantities of it through chipped paint and suffer mental impairment as a result.

9 This account of Johnson Controls' policy is drawn from the majority opinions in both the Circuit Court of Appeals and the Supreme Court. There are differences in emphasis between the two and even differences in the rendition of the facts (with the Supreme Court, for one example, not noting that Johnson Controls acquired a previously existing battery manufacturer and that the old policy was put in place by that company, and for another example, the appeals court found six pregnancies and the Supreme Court eight). The citations are: for the Circuit Court,

International Union, UAW v. Johnson Controls, Inc., 886 F. 2d 871, 875-879 (7th Cir. 1989); and for the Supreme Court, *International Union, UAW v. Johnson Controls*, 111 S. Ct. at 1200. The latter is much sketchier than the Circuit Court's opinion on the facts in the case and the details of the fetal protection policy.

In the *New York Times* article cited above (*supra* note 6), one woman who was transferred from stacking lead plates to the company laundry was still paid at the higher salary attached to her former position, although she did complain about lost bumping rights for day-shift work. Thus, it appears that Johnson Controls did make an attempt in some instances to live up to its stated policy of transferring women without loss in salary. So the record is, to say the least, somewhat contradictory, with some women claiming loss in salary upon transfer and others not.

10 The precise source of this estimate is not made clear in the EEOC citation, since the agency cited a book which in turn cited the *Washington Post*, without further identifying the original source for this estimate. The 15-20 million figure for the potential jobs that could be affected by such policies is cited in the same EEOC footnote, but here the source is identified as a Bureau of National Affairs special report issued in 1987, entitled 'Pregnancy and Employment'. Both the 100,000 and the 20 million figures are widely cited, but usually without clear attribution, or attribution to the EEOC. See: 'EEOC: Policy Statement on Reproductive and Fetal Hazards Under Title VII', October 8, 1988, at n. 2.

11 A study on such policies by the University of Massachusetts and the Massachusetts Department of Public Health identified four substances known to cause fetal harm (glycol ethers, lead, organic mercury, and inorganic mercury) and eight additional substances suspected of causing reproductive damage but for which scientific proof remains scanty (arsenic or arsine gas, benzene, carbon disulphide, formaldehyde, methylene chloride, vinyl chloride, trichloromethane or trichloroethylene, and toluene). (As cited in: 'The Battle over Fetal Protection—What's an Employer to Do?', *Fair Employment Practices*, Bureau of National Affairs, June 7, 1990, at pp. 67-8.) The study also found that of the 198 companies out of 232 that responded, only one had removal and transfer policies that applied to men.

12 'Who Decides Who Works', *supra* note 6.

13 'Justices Hear Arguments in Fetal-Protection Case', *The New York Times*, October 11, 1990.

14 *International Union v. Johnson Controls, Inc.*, 680 F. Supp. 309 (E.D. Wis. 1988).

15 Id. at 310.

16 'Summary judgment is properly entered in favor of a party when the opposing party is unable to make a showing sufficient to prove an essential element of a case on which the opposing party bears the burden of proof'. *Johnson Controls*, 886 F. 2d at 887. Granting summary judgment to Johnson Controls, thus, precluded a trial.

17 There have only been a handful of such cases. *Wright v. Olin Corporation*, 697 F. 2d 1172, at 1182 (4th Cir. 1982). This was a challenge to a fetal protection policy, similar to *Johnson Controls'*, which banned fertile women from jobs involving contact with known abortifacient or teratogenic agents. The court noted that the policy did not fit 'with absolute precision any of the developed theories, and it selected the disparate impact/business necessity paradigm that would later be accepted by the Seventh Circuit in *Johnson Controls*. *Wright* set out a three-pronged business necessity inquiry: (1) is there a substantial risk to the health of the fetus; (2) is that hazard transmitted only through women; (3) can the harm be prevented by a less discriminatory alternative. The Seventh Circuit in *Johnson Controls* would follow this mode of analysis, only differing from *Wright* in imposing the burden of persuasion on the plaintiff for all three steps. The 4th Circuit sustained the fetal protection policy in *Wright*. *Hayes v. Shelby Memorial Hospital*, 726 F. 2d 1543 (11th Cir. 1984). Here, an x-ray technician challenged her

firing by a hospital once her pregnancy was discovered. The court adopted a similar paradigm to *Wright's* of disparate impact/business necessity and the three-pronged test. The plaintiff prevailed in this case, for the court held that her firing violated Title VII because her exposure would not have risen above a limit for fetal exposure established by a Congressional advisory panel. *Zunigan v. Kleberg County Hospital*, 692 F. 2d 986 (5th Cir. 1982). This was another case of an x-ray technician fired as a result of her pregnancy; here, too, a business necessity defense was adopted by the court. After the Seventh Circuit decision and after the Supreme Court granted certiorari in *Johnson Controls*, the Sixth Circuit reversed a district court grant of summary judgment to a company with a policy similar to Johnsons', rejecting the disparate impact paradigm and viewing the only available defense as the more stringent BFOQ [see discussion in the text]. (*Grant v. General Motors Corp.*, 908 F. 2d 1303 (1990).

18 Civil Rights Act of 1964, Section 703(a); 42 U.S.C. § 2000e-2(a).

19 Title VII, § 703(e)(1).

20 *Griggs v. Duke Power Co.*, 401 U.S. 424 (1971). This is the leading case on disparate impact, setting out the theory, the elements to be proven, and the shifting burdens of proof. Recently, the Supreme Court has had another stab at refining the disparate impact theory, and its attempt has not pleased civil rights groups, for it made proving disparate impact more difficult by placing the burden of proof for all elements squarely upon the plaintiff. *Wards Cove Packing Co. v. Atonia*, 109 S.Ct. 2115 (1989). In 1990 and 1991, attempts were made in Congress to define the shifting burdens back to where they were in *Griggs*, and thus make these cases easier for plaintiffs to win, an effort that eventually succeeded.

21 *Johnson Controls*, 886 F. 2d at 908 (Easterbrook, J. dissenting).

22 Id. at 909.

23 Id. at 920.

24 Id. at 913.

25 Id.

26 Various courts have held that such additional costs of employing women as higher pension costs, or medical insurance, or more days off for sickness, or higher turnover are excluded from consideration under Title VII. Id. at 910.

27 Id. at 914.

28 Concurring opinions were filed by Justice White (joined by Chief Justice Rehnquist and Justice Kennedy) and by Justice Scalia. All of the members of the Court, however, concurred in the judgment of reversal. In Justice White's concurrence, however, he found erroneous the Court's holding that the BFOQ defense can 'never justify a sex-based fetal protection policy'. *Johnson Controls*, 111 S.Ct. at 1210 (White, J. concurring).

29 *Johnson Controls*, 111 S. Ct. at 1202.

30 Id. at 1205.

31 Id. at 1206.

32 Id. at 1207.

33 Id. at 1210.

34 Id. at 1208.

35 Tort cases of this sort would be heard in state courts, and there have been cases in which adherence to federal law has not prevented defendants from losing in state courts. Justice White, in his concurrence, lists cases in which state tort claims were not preempted by adherence to federal laws. (*See*: Id. at 1211 n. 2 (White, J. concurring)). Justice White disagreed with the Court's holding that the BFOQ defense is so narrow that a fetal protection policy could never be justified. As an example of what might qualify as a BFOQ, he argued, is a showing by an employer that in order to avoid substantial tort liability the exclusion of women from dangerous jobs is reasonably necessary.

36 *Johnson Controls*, 111 S.Ct. at 1214 (White, J. concurring).

37 Id. For an excellent account of the transformation of tort liability *see*: Peter H. Huber, *Liability: The Legal Revolution and its Consequences*, New York: Basic Books, 1988.

38 Quaintly, Judge Easterbrook repeated several times the refrain that Title VII looks to the protection of individuals rather than groups. *Johnson Controls*, 886 F. 2d at 910, 911. The judicial history of Title VII, lamentably, speaks entirely in the other direction, with group equality replacing individual equality as the standard: for an excellent discussion of how this came about see: Herman Belz, *Equality Transformed: A Quarter-Century of Affirmative Action*, Rutgers, NJ: Transaction, 1991.

39 Becker. 'From *Muller v. Oregon* to Fetal Vulnerability Policies', 53 *U. Chicago L. Rev.*, 1219 (1986).

40 208 U.S. 412 (1908).

41 Indeed, many women's groups supported such legislation in the early part of this century out of a desire to protect women from harsh conditions and long hours of labour in the workplace. Mary Becker does recognize this: *supra* note 39 at 1222 n. 10. Judge Easterbrook expresses the modern view of the old paternalism: *Johnson Controls*, 886 F. 2d at 912-3.

3

Do Women Benefit from Equal Opportunities Legislation?

David Conway

1. The Case for Equal Opportunities Legislation

Throughout the member states of the European Community as well as the USA, legislation is currently in force that prohibits discrimination in employment on grounds of sex. In all these countries, it is unlawful for an employer to select a male applicant for a post in preference to a female competitor other than on the basis of the male applicant's having superior qualifications for the post. Such legislation is comparatively new. It bears testament to the enormous and ever-growing influence which feminist ideology has come to enjoy in every department of public life within the last several decades.

It is widely believed by its supporters that, on its own, such legislation stops well short of securing all that justice demands on behalf of women in matters connected with work. Even when it has succeeded in putting an end to sex discrimination at the point of selection, women are said to remain unfairly handicapped in competition for jobs with men unless further legislative measures are taken. This is said for two closely related reasons. The first is that pregnancy and child-bearing are in themselves incapacitating to some degree. Temporarily, at least, they impair a woman's ability to work. Second, traditionally, primary responsibility for looking after infants and children has fallen to their biological mothers.

Typically, women who have children are obliged to withdraw, at least temporarily, from full-time paid employment in order to bear and look after them in their early years. This is in marked contrast with men whose full-time availability for work is nothing like as adversely affected by becoming fathers. The interruption to the full-time working lives of women arising from their becoming mothers causes them to fall behind their male counterparts so far as employment prospects are concerned. It obliges such women to miss out on the acquisition of job-experience and job-related skills which their male counterparts acquire in consequence of not being obliged to cease full-time work on becoming a parent. Additionally, during these intervals from full-time work, such women must forgo opportunities for promotion and other forms of career advancement which present themselves to their male counterparts who suffer no correspondingly severe impediments to full-time work.

These handicaps in the employment stakes imposed on women by their becoming mothers survive unscathed the introduction of legislation prohibiting sex discrimination at the point of job selection. Even where a woman starts off her working career with equal qualifications and skills to a man, and can compete with him in job application on fully equal terms, she is liable to start to fall behind him in terms of job prospects upon becoming a mother. A woman who must temporarily withdraw from the labour market in consequence of motherhood will, as a result, cease to remain as well qualified and able to advance her career as an initially no better skilled and qualified man.

It is a widely shared sentiment that it is unfair on women who wish to have children that they alone should be obliged to bear all the costs which their having children imposes upon their earnings capacity. Further legal measures beyond prohibiting sex discrimination in job selection are therefore deemed necessary to secure full equity for women in the realm of work. Such measures range from statutory maternity leave with full pay, to tax allowances on child-care for working mothers, and so on. The general governing principle behind all such recommendations is that no woman should be subject to any handicap in employment to which men are not equally subject. The realm of employment should be gender-blind.

2. The Opportunity Costs of Equal Opportunities

The introduction of legislation to promote equal opportunities at work for the two sexes is not without substantial economic costs, a reality not always appreciated by advocates of the legislation. There is, first, the cost in terms of lost production that would otherwise occur if labour did not need to be expended, in monitoring and enforcing the legislation. Second, and more importantly, compliance with the legislative measures itself adds significantly and directly to the costs of production.

To illustrate how great the direct economic costs of compliance can be, consider a simplified model consisting of a husband, Adam, and wife, Eve, who live together on a farm, producing bushels of wheat for sale on the open market. Suppose, for the sake of argument, that, initially at least, Adam and Eve are equally skilled and competent in wheat production both producing the same amount of wheat in same amount of time. However, it is Eve not Adam who bears their children. Because the acts of bearing and nurturing a child reduce a woman's capacity to engage in other forms of activity, in any year in which Eve has children, therefore, Adam will be capable of engaging in wheat production for more days than Eve. Let us further suppose that wheat production is an activity of which it is true that the more days that an individual engages in it, the more skilled and hence more productive that individual becomes.

Consider two alternative ways in which Adam and Eve can effect a division of labour between them, judged from the standpoint of aggregate output measured in terms of bushels of wheat. First, there is what can be called a *gender-based* division:

> Adam concentrates exclusively on producing wheat, and Eve alone attends to the domestic chores and child-minding, only working in the fields in any time left over.

The second form of division can be called *ungendered*:

> Adam and Eve divide equally between them the domestic and agricultural tasks. Adam spends the morning in the fields and in the afternoon minds the children and does household chores. Conversely, Eve spends the mornings at

56

home child-minding and doing domestic chores, and works in the fields in the afternoons.

Which form of division of labour achieves greater output for Adam and Eve? Given the assumptions of the case, the answer is obvious that it is the gender-based division.

This two-person farm may be considered a microcosm of society at large. The two forms of division of labour correspond respectively with those form of sexual division of labour which would spontaneously tend to emerge in the absence and in the presence of equal opportunities legislation (provided that women choose to avail themselves of the career opportunities opened up by it).

Consider a society, like our own, which pursues equal opportunities for women through legislative measures, such as prohibiting sex discrimination in selection, recruitment, and training, requiring paid maternity leave, granting the right to equal pay, and so on. The sexual division of labour in such a society is bound through time more closely to become less gender-based and more ungendered.

Many who favour equal opportunities measures complain that current legislation has not yet fully succeeded in bringing about this desired result. Instead, all too often, women who avail themselves of the job opportunities these measures have created find themselves having to combine their working-careers with the household work traditionally associated with women. Their male partners continue to focus exclusively on their work much as before. However, so it will be said, equal opportunities measures have not yet fully caught hold. When they do, it will turn out that child-minding and other domestic chores will come to be more equitably distributed between men and women.

Consider, by contrast, the form of sexual division of labour that is likely to emerge in a society in which employers are legally free to discriminate on grounds of sex in job appointments. Consider an employer in the process of selecting an applicant for a job, and faced with a choice between a male and an equally qualified but fertile female applicant. Assuming that the employer has no intrinsic preference for either sex but wishes merely to maximise profits, the employer is likely to select the male in preference to the female applicant. This is because, other things being equal, a female employee of child-bearing capacity is more likely to withdraw from employment, or be otherwise less available for work, than a male counterpart. This is as a result of the likelihood of her becoming pregnant at some point in her working career.

Hiring a woman, when an equally well-qualified man was available, would be an unsound economic move for any employer looking to make a long-term appointment. These alone can reap the full benefits of any job-training which have to be given in the initial years to an employee. Given the higher likelihood of the woman being less available for work than the man in consequence of her becoming pregnant at some point, the appointment of a fertile woman in preference to an equally qualified man would be an unsound economic decision for any employer. A society which permits sex discrimination in employment, therefore, will tend to a sexual division of labour that is more gender-based than ungendered.

If the foregoing assumptions are sound, and if one is merely concerned with maximising aggregate output, it would appear that current equal opportunities legislation is causing society to produce less wealth than it would do in the absence of such legislation.

3. Equity and Gender

Advocates of equal opportunities legislation are unlikely to be much impressed by the foregoing considerations. They are likely to respond by saying that considerations of aggregate output are beside the point. What is at issue, so they will say, is equity between the sexes. So far as that is concerned, it is not so important how much society produces by the adoption of some given form of sexual division of labour. Rather, what matters is how that output is divided up between the sexes. The consequence of prohibiting sex discrimination in employment may well be to make the aggregate national output lower than it would be were such discrimination permitted. On the other hand, so it will be maintained, the *shares* of the national output that go to the respective sexes will be very different under the two different forms of division of labour. When equal opportunities legislation is in force, it will be claimed, women will, in practice, command a far larger share of the national output than they would without the legislation. Even if the size of the national cake is smaller than it would otherwise be, justice demands the legislation.

Men undoubtedly end up with less for themselves under equal opportunities legislation than they would in its absence. However, they could not reasonably complain of suffering any injustice at the hands of such legislation, if they end up with it no worse than women would be without it. Men end up with the lion's share of the aggregate national output when sex discrimination is permitted in employment. Hence, it will be said, men and women both fare better under equal opportunities legislation than women do where it is not there to prevent discrimination against them in employment. Men cannot justifiably complain of being hard done by in being made to enjoy less than they otherwise would do. For such legislation still leaves them appreciably better off than women would be were employers free to practice sex discrimination.

4. Equity Without Equal Opportunity

Suppose it could be established that women are better off where equal opportunities legislation is in force than they are when employers can and do practice sex discrimination in favour of men. Suppose it could be furthered established that, in such circumstances, men are better off than women are where such legislation is absent. Even if these suppositions are made, it still does not follow that equity requires or even permits such legislation. This is because it is possible to envisage circumstances in which sex discrimination in employment is permitted in law and is widely practised as a result, but in which nonetheless both men and women end up appreciably better off than either would be were equal opportunities legislation in force.

To see what these circumstances might be, let us return to our two-peopled farm model. Let us suppose that with a gender-based division of labour the daily output of wheat is 100 bushels and that with an ungendered division it is 90.

Anyone who supposes that greater equity for Eve is secured by means of an ungendered rather than a gender-based division of labour with Adam is tacitly supposing that the benefits of the proceeds of sale of the output produced by the farm go exclusively, or at least preponderantly, to the immediate producer of that output. If the farm is to be at all viable under the gender-based division of labour, Eve must end up enjoying some of the benefits of the proceeds of sale of the wheat produced by Adam. For the sake of argument, suppose that Adam and Eve disburse the benefits of the proceeds of sale between them in accordance with the following rule:

> For every bushel of wheat produced by any partner, that partner keeps 50 per cent of the proceeds of sale, and divides the remaining 50 per cent in equal measure with the other partner, or else puts it to use from which both gain equal benefit.

When distribution of benefits is in accordance with this rule, Adam and Eve respectively end up under each form of division of labour with relative benefits as follows:

Division of Labour	Aggregate Output	Adam	Eve
Gender-Based	100	75	25
Ungendered	90	45	45

If the only possible way of effecting a distribution of output is in accordance with a rule like the above that favours the immediate producer of it, then Eve would be better off with an ungendered than with a gender-based division of labour. Moreover, under the same supposition, Adam would be better off with an ungendered division of labour than Eve is where the division is gender-based. Suppose a choice had to be made by Adam and Eve between one or other of the two forms of division of labour, assuming both preferred one or other of these forms to no form of co-operation between them. And assume that there would be no co-operation unless agreement on a form of division of labour was reached. Adam could hardly have any grounds for refusing to accept an ungendered-division. Although he ends up with less under it than he does under the gender-based division, Eve would end up under the gender-based division with still less than that. Assume that both parties agree that the interests of neither should be sacrificed for those of the other. Then, provided the only possible distributive rule was some rule favouring producers, the form of division of labour that would be chosen by both parties would be ungendered. Neither party could have any legitimate cause to complain about the adoption of this form of sexual division of labour in preference to the gender-based division. By contrast, Eve would have legitimate cause to complain that her interests were being sacrificed for the sake of Adam's were the gender-based division adopted. Consequently, it would seem that, granted all the assumptions above, justice between Adam and Eve is achieved when and only when they adopt an ungendered division of labour between them.

5. The Real World

If one extrapolates to the real world, then it would seem, by parity of reasoning, that, despite the loss of output that results from equal opportunities legislation, considerations of equity between the sexes demand such legislation. This, of course, is provided that in the real world, in the absence of such legislation, women are worse off than men are when such legislation is in force. This is what is said by those who support equal opportunities legislation. Men do not suffer from such legislation as much as women suffer from the lack of it.

Such a conclusion can be safely drawn from the model, however, only if a further supposition is made. This is that, were all equal opportunities legislation rescinded, and were there to (re)emerge in consequence a more gender-based division of labour than obtains where such legislation is in force, men and women could not both be better off than they either could both be without it. This supposition would be correct, however, only if it were not possible to disburse the benefits of production other than in accordance with a distributive rule favouring producers of the sort earlier considered.

It has been argued above that, given that initially Adam and Eve possess equal strength and skill, a gender-based division of labour will result in greater aggregate output than would be attained by means of an ungendered division of labour, if they are to have children. What makes this true are the laws of production. These laws of production are fixed and unalterable by human decision. However, as John Stuart Mill long ago observed,[1] laws governing the distribution of output are not likewise fixed and immutable. In consequence, a rule that favours producers is not the only possible rule in accordance with which we may suppose that output is capable of being divided between Adam and Eve. Besides it, there alternative possible rules which would leave both Adam and Eve better off under a gender-based division of labour than both would be capable of being left under any other possible form of division of labour and method of distributing output between them.

Consider the most obvious of such alternative rules:

Any partner who produces a bushel of wheat divides the benefits of the proceeds of sale of that bushel equally with the other partner.

When the benefits of production are divided up in accordance with this rule, then the resultant benefits to each party of the two forms of division of labour are as follows:

Division of Labour	Aggregate Output	Adam	Eve
Gender-Based	100	50	50
Ungendered	90	45	45

Where the benefits of the sale of output are distributed between Adam and Eve in accordance with this rule, then a gender-based division of labour yields both Adam and Eve more than an ungendered division of labour can yield both.

6. Optimising Women's Welfare without Equal Opportunities

How does such a conclusion extrapolate to the real world? One important lesson that may be drawn is that equal opportunities legislation need not necessarily be the best way to promote the welfare of women, let alone that of men. Recent studies[2] have revealed that the principal reason why married women work is to increase income. Given this to be so, whether equal opportunities legislation benefits women turns ultimately on whether it puts such a constraint on production as to render both men and women less well-off than they both would, or at least could, be without it. This would be so only if, in its absence, the benefits of the greater output that would result would be disbursed between the sexes in a manner that favours producers over their domestically occupied partners.

Supporters of the legislation will, of course, be likely to respond by saying that, before it was introduced, the distribution of the benefits of production between the sexes left women with less than they would have had were such legislation to have brought about a more equal distribution of earnings between the two sexes.

However, the considerations which are invariably cited in support of this contention do not in fact bear it out. Two considerations tend to be cited above all. The first is the lower average earnings which women have traditionally enjoyed as compared with men. This is cited as 'proof' that the distribution of the benefits of aggregate production is less favourable to women than it would be were equal opportunities in employment fully achieved. However, the fact that men earn more than women do in the absence of such legislation does not suffice in itself to show that women would be better off for its introduction. The deleterious effects which it undoubtedly has on production might well be so great as to leave both sexes worse off than either would be were there to be no such legislation.

The second most commonly cited consideration in support of the contention that women fare better with equal opportunities legislation than they do without it is the alleged inequitable power relations which men are said to enjoy over women when the former are the primary income earners in a family and the latter the primary caretakers. It is said that this form of domestic division of labour gives men a power over women which enables them to gain more from the arrangement than their spouses can and more than they would have under the ungendered sexual division of labour that would tend to arise under equal opportunities.

It is less than certain, however, that men have enjoyed or must enjoy more power over their spouses than these spouses have over their husbands. At least, it is doubtful men did from the time full legal and political rights were granted to women and once suitable adjustments were made to divorce laws.

Suppose, as is the case, that the established legal practice in cases of divorce is for the courts, other things being equal, to grant care of the children to the mother whilst requiring the father to pay maintenance. Under these circumstances, there is no reason to suppose that being the primary wage earner in a family gives the man more power over his wife than she has over him.

It seems fairly uncontentious to suppose that, other things being equal, a father will prefer to be domiciled with his children and their mother than not, if he must maintain them all irrespective of whether he is domiciled with them. Where wives enjoy custody of children upon divorce and where fathers are obliged upon divorce to maintain their ex-wives and children, the threat of possible divorce by a wife may be presumed to act as a powerful deterrent against the husband choosing to let his wife enjoy a less than equitable share of the benefits of his earnings.

Suppose a married woman considered that her marital partner provided her with insufficient of his earnings to compensate her fully for the handicap to her earnings-potential that would arise from her sex in a society which was free to practise sex discrimination in employment. She need not necessarily be any worse off in the absence than in the presence of equal opportunities legislation. She would not be worse off in its absence, provided wives possess the legal right to separate and eventually divorce their husbands, and be maintained by them, on the grounds that their husbands have provided them with less than an equitable share of the benefits of their joint income. This proviso will be sufficient to safeguard the interests of married women, if they have had to incur any sacrifice to their earnings capacity in consequence of marriage and if their primary purpose in working is financial. That men take home the bulk of the family income in their pay-packets does not, therefore, mean that they are effectively guaranteed any more of the benefits of that income than their wives. Further legal protection for women than currently exists is possible that stops well short of equal opportunities. For example, one mechanism to which the state could resort to ensure that mothers did not receive insufficient from the fathers of their children would be a system of child benefit allowances linked to the income of the fathers and financed from taxation on his income. No doubt there are still other possibilities.

7. Contracts of Employment

There is one class of women who might be thought to end up with less than they would in the absence of equal opportunities legislation. This would be so no matter how generous men were to their spouses. These are women who might prefer not to have children and who might be thought to be losers in a system which permitted employers to discriminate against women on the grounds of their expected lesser earnings capacity due to maternity. Is it true, however, that nothing short of equal opportunities legislation can prevent them from being unfairly discriminated against? The answer again is: no. One possible way in which their interests could be fully protected without resort to the cumbersome and costly device of equal opportunities legislation would be the legalisation of contracts of employment, presently proscribed by equal opportunities law as being unfairly discriminatory to women, which required female employees to agree to forgo having children for stipulated periods. In case this is thought to be a vicious form of contract, it should be observed that at the moment we are only considering women who choose not to have children. For them, entering into such a contract does not constitute any sacrifice.

It might be objected that some women would not know at an early stage of their career whether they would want to have children. They may be tempted to sign such contracts for the sake of the higher remuneration they would bring and then come to regret their decision. Well, contracts can be devised to take account of these possibilities: for example, it might be part of the contract that, in the event of the woman deciding she wants to have children, she must work for a finite period, at a much lower salary before being free to leave. And no doubt there are many more possible ways round such problem-cases. The general point remains sound. Equal opportunities legislation is almost certainly not the best way to protect and further the interests of women. It imposes costs on all that are not, or need not be, outweighed by the benefits some women obtain from such legislation.

8. How To Achieve Equity Between The Sexes Without Equal Opportunities

It might still be felt that women must be unfairly disadvantaged in comparison with men, so long as it remains the case that their career prospects are more adversely affected than men's are by their becoming parents. It is difficult for some to shake off the thought that equity between the sexes demands that those impediments to the pursuit of careers that are the unavoidable consequence of having children should be distributed equally between the two sexes, and that such equalisation can only be effected by means of the full panoply of equal opportunities legislation. It is understandable that things can appear this way to many, but it is still a mistaken impression, as recourse to the simplified model farm reveals.

Suppose the children of Adam and Eve have grown up and left the farm. Suppose also, as was previously assumed, that skill at wheat production increases with experience in the task. It will follow under these two suppositions that the adoption of a gender-based division of labour will have made Eve a less skilled wheat-producer than she would have become had they adopted an ungendered division of labour between them during their family-raising years. Would not Eve, judged over the full period of her working life, have been better off with the ungendered than with the gender-based division of labour? After the children have left the farm and she wishes to resume her work in the fields, possibly on a farm of her own, will she not have become a less skilled wheat-producer than she would have become had she and Adam adopted an ungendered division of labour?

There are two possibilities here that require separate consideration: first, Adam and Eve are happy with each other and want to continue to live together as a couple after the children have grown up; second, Eve cannot wait for the day she no longer need be responsible for the children and cannot wait to see the last of Adam.

Where Adam and Eve are a happy couple, the fact that, after her child-bearing years, Eve ends up under the gender-based division of labour a less skilled-wheat producer than she would have ended up had she and Adam adopted an ungendered division of labour does not in any way demonstrate that she has been subject by the gender-based division of labour to any unfair disadvantage in comparison with Adam. For had the division of labour between them been ungendered, then Adam would not have become nearly as skilled as he does at wheat production. Since, it has been assumed that they share equally in the benefits of their joint income and it is for the sake of that income they each work, Eve ends up under the gender-based division of labour better off, though less skilled at wheat production, than she would had the division of labour been ungendered.

In the case where Adam and Eve are an unhappy couple, and where Eve wants to separate from Adam and go her own way, will not a gender-based division of labour have unfairly disadvantaged her relative to Adam? Again, the answer is: not necessarily. It is true that, because of the gender-based division of labour they have adopted, Adam has acquired all the human capital in terms of skill at wheat production and Eve none. It is also true that, upon separating after they have raised their family, Eve would have ended up more skilled at wheat production had the division of labour been ungendered rather than gender-based. However, Eve need not end up unfairly disadvantaged in comparison with Adam at the termination of their relationship together after they had adopted the gender-based division. They would both end up better off with the gender-based division than with the ungendered division, and neither would be unfairly disadvantaged relative to each other, provided, at the time of the termination of their partnership, Eve is fully compensated for the loss to her own earnings potential she sustained in virtue of their having chosen a gender-based division in preference to the ungendered division. She would be fully compensated if she were to receive an equal share of the benefits of the additional productivity that, at the time of separation, Adam possesses in consequence of having previously worked under a gender-based than with an ungendered division of labour. This may well require that Eve has an entitlement to a share of the future income of Adam after they have separated, or else that Eve is entitled to a greater share of the joint assets at the time of separation. Provided the terms under which they dissolve their partnership satisfy these conditions, then neither party is unfairly disadvantaged by the previous gender-based division of labour and both benefit from it more than they would from an ungendered division.

9. Conclusion

Extrapolating once again to the real world, the final conclusion must be that it is in the divorce courts and family courts and not in the workplace that the law should be used to achieve equity between the sexes.

In the final analysis, there is at most only one set of people who benefit from equal opportunities legislation: those who campaign for it and who administer the monitoring and enforcement of it. No doubt they will be the hardest to convince that such laws are not necessary to secure justice for women. Fortunately, the final decision whether there be such legislation does not rest in their hands.

68

Notes

1 Mill writes: 'The laws and conditions of the production of wealth, partake of the character of physical truths. There is nothing optional, or arbitrary in them. Whether ...[mankind] ...like it or nor not, their production will be limited by the amount of their previous accumulation, and, that being given, it will be proportional to their energy, their skill, the perfection of their machinery, and their judicious use of the advantages of combined labour.... It is not so with the Distribution of Wealth. That is a matter of human institution only.... The distribution of wealth, therefore, depends on the laws and customs of society.' John Stuart Mill, *Principles of Political Economy*, Book 11, ch. 1, s.1. (1871 Edition), Donald Winch (ed), Harmondsworth: Penguin, 1970, pp. 349-50.

2 See Jean Martin and Ceridwen Roberts, *Women and Employment: A Lifetime Perspective*, London: Her Majesty's Stationary Office, 1984. This book is a report of a national survey of women carried out in 1980 jointly by the Department of Employment and the Office of Population Censuses and Surveys. The authors write: 'When asked to select a main reason for working..., respondents showed clearly the importance of financial reasons.... 69 per cent mentioned a financial reason as their main reason for working', p. 68.

4

Women, Work and Well-Being

Ivy Papps

1. Introduction

Legislation for equal pay and equal opportunities in the workplace were major objectives of the Women's Movement from its inception in the 1960s, illustrating the importance placed on the labour force by those concerned with improving women's lives. In addition, the female labour force participation rate has consistently been used as an indicator of women's position with the implication that high levels of participation are connected with high status.

There are two basic assumptions behind this idea. First, it is assumed that increased participation reflects greater opportunities for women. Second, it is assumed that individuals who earn money income have better access to resources and more freedom in consumption. Thus, for both reasons, it is assumed that an increased female labour force participation rate makes women better off because they have access to more resources and have more freedom of choice in the allocation of these resources.

This chapter will challenge both these assumptions. Section 2 will use some elementary economic ideas to examine the relationship between women's well-being and increases in the female labour force participation rate. It will show that the impact of labour force activity on women depends on the factors which have caused the change and that, therefore, the female labour force participation rate does not provide an unambiguous indicator of women's position. Section 3 illustrates the argument with data from OECD countries although it should be stressed at this point that the data used are not entirely satisfactory and should be considered only as illustrative. Section 4 discusses the policy implications.

2. *The Economics of the Labour Market*

In most countries, most adults work full-time although, if we consider the world as a whole, most do not receive money wages for their work. Many workers produce goods and services for direct consumption by their families by working on land which is owned or rented by a member of the family; process, preserve and prepare food in the family kitchen; spin, weave and sew raw materials to make clothes and furnishings; build, improve or maintain their homes; bear and rear children. Although many readers will consider non-market production a characteristic of less developed countries, the short list above makes it clear that a great deal of non-market production also occurs in modern developed economies. Thus, for most adults, the choice is not whether or not to work but what kind of work to do. The conventional arguments outlined in the first section are based essentially on the idea that it is work for money wages which improves women's position and this section develops the analysis in terms of the market for waged labour.

Elementary economic theory tells us that wages and the level of employment are determined by the forces of supply and demand. The greater is the demand for a particular kind of labour, because of an increase in its productivity for example, the greater will be both the level of employment and the returns to that labour (the wage). On the other hand, an increase in the supply of labour, by means of labour migration for example, will reduce the wage although it will also increase the level of employment. Thus, an increase in both the supply of and the demand for labour will increase the level of employment but these increases have very different implications for the wage.

The main argument of this chapter is, therefore, that it is the returns to work which are of most importance for women's position since the argument is based on the command over real resources obtained by working women. Thus, the relevant labour market indicator is the wage not the level of employment. The use of participation rates as an indicator of women's position contains the implicit assumption that the level of employment and the returns to labour are positively related. If this were so, the female labour force participation rate which is relatively easily observed[1] may be used as a proxy for the returns to labour which are more difficult to identify because of the widespread existence of non-pecuniary costs and benefits of various jobs due to varying working conditions and fringe benefits. Unfortunately, however, it is implausible to assume that all differences in participation rates are a result of differences in demand; some may be due to differences in supply.

This simple analysis makes it possible to disentangle some of the discussion about working women which seems at first to be contradictory. Although there is a widespread belief that higher levels of female labour force participation imply that women are better off, there is a substantial body of literature which recognises that working women do at least two jobs because they accept the major part of domestic responsibilities and, therefore, work very much harder than women who do not do paid work.[2] Thus, on the one hand women who do paid work are thought to be better off because they control more resources, while on the other hand they are thought to be worse off because they work longer hours. We may now see that those who stress the benefits may have in their minds the benefits of increased choice derived from an increased demand for women's work while those who stress the disadvantages may be considering the pressures on women to increase the supply of their labour.

An important factor contributing to differences in supply is the level of income. Many empirical studies[3] of labour supply find that individuals with lower incomes choose to work more than those with higher incomes who are otherwise in the same circumstances. If we extrapolate this result to the national level, we may infer that richer countries would have a lower female labour force participation rate than poorer countries. Of course, we do not usually observe such a relationship. The US has a higher female labour force participation rate than India and European countries have generally higher rates than countries in the Middle East. However, these countries differ in ways other than levels of income. They have different economic structures and different labour productivity which results in different relative rewards from working in the waged sector rather than in subsistence activities. Thus, a simple comparison between countries in terms of income is not sufficient to invalidate the observation that lower incomes increase the supply of labour. In such a case, a higher female labour force participation rate will be associated with lower returns for working women.

The Female Labour Force Participation Rate

To emphasise this elementary point, let us consider how the government could increase the female labour force participation rate in the UK. One method which is likely to prove highly effective given the evidence about the reaction of the supply of women workers to changes in income is the abolition of all forms of income transfers such as unemployment pay, child benefit and Supplementary Benefit. The large fall in income experienced by the poorer members of society would increase the willingness of women in those families to work for money wages.

The female labour force participation rate would rise but these women would, of course, be worse off and it would be foolish to advocate such a policy. The female labour force participation rate is, therefore, likely to be a very unsatisfactory measure of the position of women in a country. This point is important for two reasons:

1. Much policy discussion is based on the premise that an increase in the female labour force participation rate reflects an improvement in women's position and, therefore, policy is directed toward measures to increase that rate. Since some of these measures are essentially subsidies to female employment (for example, free or subsidised nursery provision) which are intended to have a redistributive effect,[4] it would be helpful to ask whether the same subsidy could be provided in a more effective way—by an income transfer, for example.[5]

2. If policies intended to improve women's position are evaluated by means of the female labour force participation rate, an improvement may be inferred when the true situation is that women are worse off because of some factor, such as a fall in income, which has increased the supply of their labour.

Returns to Labour

The main policy issue should not be the method of production nor how many people earn money wages but the value of resources controlled by the individuals concerned. With no constraints on data collection, the observation in which we were interested would be the returns to labour earned by those employed. This observation would provide information, not only about the resources controlled by those working in the labour market but also about the resources controlled by those working in the non-monetised sector, since those individuals will only choose not to work in the monetised sector if they can obtain commensurate returns in the non-monetised sector.

Unfortunately, however, the returns to labour are very difficult to observe directly. Data on wage rates and/or earnings can only be collected by means of sample surveys because the questionnaires necessary to collect reasonably accurate data are too detailed to be administered to the whole population. This kind of data collection is a very expensive process and there are, therefore, a number of countries for which they are not available. Moreover, even if these data were available, they would not provide good information about the returns to labour because they omit information about conditions of work (danger and unpleasantness, for example) and non-monetary or indirect payments such as fringe benefits. These factors are important for the policy issue, which is concerned with the well-being of the people concerned.

In addition, an average measure of the returns to labour may be highly misleading because workers differ in the level of skills they possess and, generally, more skilled workers are the first to be drawn into the labour force. The higher is the demand for labour the more incentive there will be for lower skilled individuals to enter the labour market. Workers already in the labour force will be able to earn higher wages (because of the increased demand) while new workers will earn wages higher than those which they could have earned before (which is what has encouraged them to join the labour force) although they will probably earn less than the workers originally in the labour force. Such entry will, therefore, lower the average returns to labour even though all individuals in the labour market are better off.[6]

There are, therefore, considerable difficulties encountered in using a single measure drawn from the labour market as an indicator of women's position. An alternative approach is to bypass the labour market and to attempt to derive direct measures of well-being. A crude measure of well-being may be derived from indices of health. We know, for example, that poor people have generally worse health than richer people even in developed countries.[7] Although some of these differences may be due to life-style, it is likely that some are also due to differences in access to resources.[8] Thus, while it is important to realise that health is the outcome of a number of choices, the evidence we have provides some indication that it appears to be related to the amount of resources available to individuals.

3. Female Labour Force Participation and Women's Well-Being

Table 1 presents some basic socio-economic data for twenty four OECD countries. It is worth noting first of all that the average wage rate for men and women is available for fewer than half the countries emphasising the point made earlier about the difficulties encountered in collecting this information. There is no obvious connection in this table between the female labour force participation rate and female life expectancy and Figure 1[9] confirms this impression.[10] Indeed, the two countries with the highest and lowest life expectancy (Switzerland and Portugal) have virtually the same female labour force participation rates approximately equal to the average rate. However, as argued above, there appears to be a considerably stronger relationship between life expectancy and income as demonstrated for women in Figure 2.[11] Thus, differences across countries in resources available to individuals does seem to be reflected in differences in life expectancy and there appears to be some justification for using female life expectancy as an indicator of women's socio-economic position.

However, the argument so far is much too simple because it concentrates on women's absolute position while the political debate refers to their position relative to that of men. It is clear from Table 1 that there are differences across countries for men and, moreover, men's life expectancy is everywhere less than that of women. The previous argument could lead one to the conclusion that women had access to more resources in all countries under discussion. However, it is well-known that women appear to possess some genetic factors which improve their survival possibilities for a given level of resources. In addition, labour force participation of both men and women may be affected by common factors. Therefore, Figure 3 shows values of relative life expectancy and relative labour force participation[12] for the twenty three OECD countries for which the data are available. Again, there appears to be no connection between women's labour force participation and their well-being.[13] On the other hand, Figure 4 shows relative life expectancy and relative wages for the nine countries for which the wage data are available and here the relationship is fairly strong.[14] Thus, although there appears to be no relationship between women's well-being and their participation in the labour market, there does appear to be some connection between their well-being and their relative command over resources which they obtain from their work in spite of the caveats about the use of the wage rate as an indicator of the returns to labour which were discussed in the last section.

4. Some Policy Implications

If the relationship between women's well-being and their participation in the paid labour force is so tenuous, then this analysis calls into question the efficacy of a number of conventional policies which have increases in female labour force participation as their primary objective. Perhaps more important, by concentrating on the mechanics of the labour market, this analysis makes it possible to assess a number of policies more carefully.

The general proposition to be drawn from an analysis of the labour market is that women will be made better off by policies which make them more attractive to potential employers and conversely will be made worse off by policies which make them less attractive. While this may seem an obvious point, it is often ignored in the discussion of labour market policies.

Consider, for example, the case of maternity benefits. The conventional view of such benefits is that they make women better off because women are partially compensated for the loss in labour market earnings which they experience as a result of bearing children. There is little systematic discussion of the impact of such maternity benefits on the operation of the labour market and, in particular, it is seldom recognised[15] that the effects of such benefits depend on who is responsible for financing these benefits. If employers are responsible, then they will view such 'benefits' in the same way as they would view a tax on female employment. They would be less willing to employ women workers and the demand for women workers would fall. Thus, the returns to work would fall for women workers.[16]

However, if the government financed the benefits, they would have the same effect as a subsidy to women workers and would tend to increase both the level of employment and the returns to working women.[17] Unfortunately, however, it is impossible to examine this proposition empirically within the scope of this chapter. Information on maternity benefits in the countries under consideration are difficult to obtain on a systematic basis and the regulations are in many cases so complex that a great deal of work would be required in order to test these ideas. Such testing remains a subject for future research.

More generally, the implication of this analysis is that policy makers concerned with improving the position of women should be seeking policies which increase the demand for women workers. Thus, the concentration on the supply of female labour, although it is of some importance for other areas of policy, is largely irrelevant for this particular purpose. The factors which draw women into the paid labour force are of academic interest, but have little to offer to discussions of policies aimed at improving the position of women. However, the size of the reaction of the supply of female labour to changes in demand will determine the impact of the policy on women's well-being and will have some importance for estimating the cost-effectiveness of the policy.[18]

Conclusions

This chapter has argued that the conventional emphasis on the female labour force participation rate is misplaced because it ignores the operation of the labour market. Policy makers who wish to improve the position of women by intervention in the labour market should seek policies which increase the demand for women workers and should judge the efficacy of their policies by reference to indicators which measure directly the control over resources enjoyed by women rather than by reference to the female labour force participation rate. This chapter used a crude measure of the resources obtained by women (the female life expectancy) and found that in a comparison among OECD countries this measure provided a reasonable indication of the command over real resources in the aggregate. However, there appeared to be little relationship between this measure and the female labour force participation rate and we may conclude that differences in female labour force participation are due to differences in the supply of women workers as well as differences in demand.

The data used in this chapter and the methods used to analyse them are far too crude to be conclusive. It is common for academics to conclude that more research is necessary but, in order to develop policies aimed at improving the lot of half the population, it is important that policy discussions be based on a firmer theoretical and empirical base than has so far been the case.

Table 1

Some Socio-Economic Indicators
OECD Countries, 1980s

	Labour Force Participation Rate		Life Expectancy (Years)		Wage Rate (US$ per hour)		Income (US$ per capita)
	Men	Women	Men	Women	Men	Women	
Japan	87.1	58.4	75.6	81.4	15.43	10.00	23,317
Belgium	72.5	51.4	70.0	76.8	8.89	6.66	15,364
Denmark	90.3	78.3	71.8	77.6	16.04	13.22	20,136
France	75.4	55.7	72.0	80.3	7.22	5.88	16,999
Germany	82.6	54.4	71.8	78.4	10.82	7.97	19,742
Luxembourg	88.2	47.6	70.0	76.0	87.58	57.59	19,169
Netherlands	79.4	50.6	73.0	79.6	10.62	8.09	15,400
UK	87.2	63.5	71.2	77.5	6.54	4.54	14,589
New Zealand	82.9	62.0	71.0	77.3	7.99	6.46	10,202
Canada	85.4	66.6	78.3	79.8	N/A	N/A	18,171
US	85.5	66.9	71.3	78.3	N/A	N/A	19,813
Austria	80.3	53.7	75.5	78.1	N/A	N/A	15,758
Finland	80.8	73.0	70.5	78.7	N/A	N/A	17,906
Greece	75.8	41.7	72.2	76.4	N/A	N/A	5,204
Ireland	83.9	37.6	70.1	75.6	N/A	N/A	8,097
Italy	78.8	43.9	71.4	78.1	N/A	N/A	13,102
Portugal	84.7	59.1	68.4	75.2	N/A	N/A	3,833
Turkey	78.3	45.8	62.5	65.8	N/A	N/A	1,341
Australia	84.8	59.0	72.8	79.1	N/A	N/A	14,431
Norway	87.2	72.8	72.8	79.6	N/A	N/A	21,232
Spain	77.3	39.4	72.5	78.6	N/A	N/A	8,615
Sweden	84.4	80.1	74.1	80.2	N/A	N/A	21,155
Switzerland	94.2	57.9	73.8	80.5	N/A	N/A	29,676
Iceland	N/A	N/A	74.0	80.2	N/A	N/A	22,874

Note: N/A—Not available

Sources: IMF International Financial Statistics XXXXIII.4 (1989)

ILO Yearbook of Labour Statistics 1989-90

OECD Labour Force Statistics 1968-88

UN Demographic Yearbook 1988

Figure 1. Life Expectancy and Labour Force Particpation

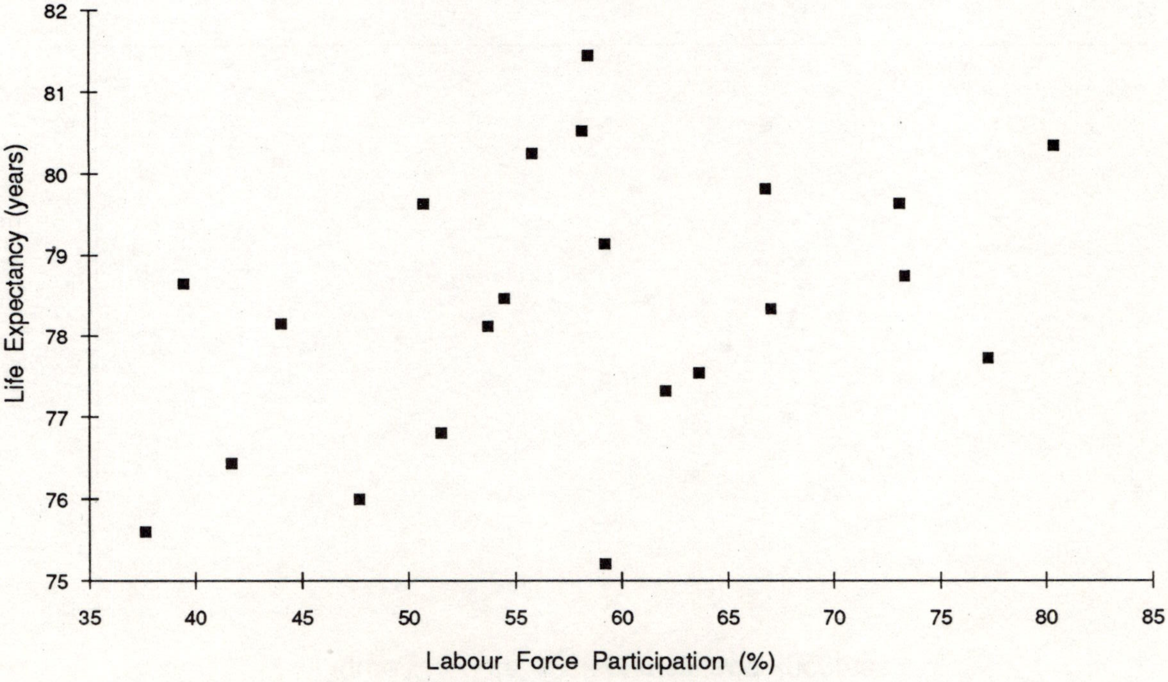

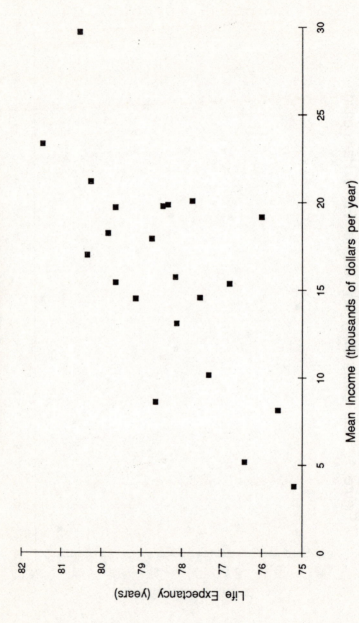

Figure 2. Life Expectancy and Incomes

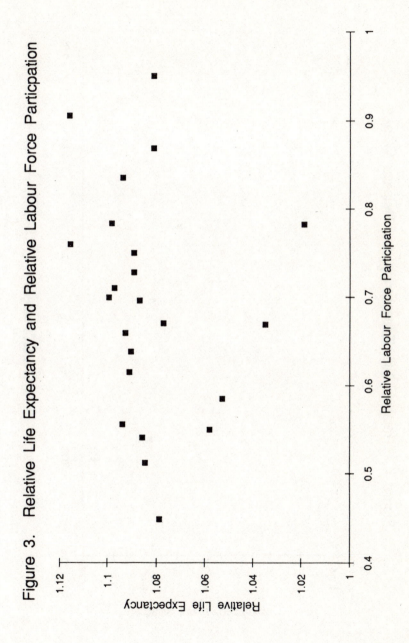

Figure 3. Relative Life Expectancy and Relative Labour Force Particpation

Figure 4. Relative Life Expectancy and Relative Wages

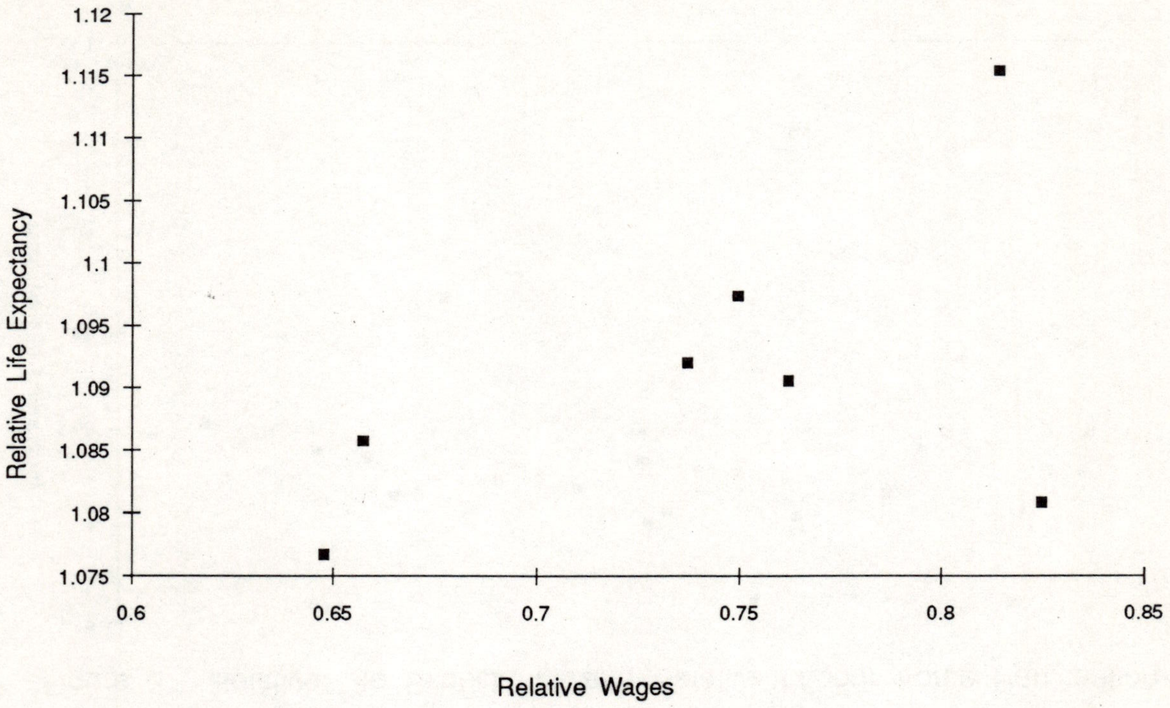

References

Birks, J.S., Papps, I., and Sinclair, C.A., 'Expansion of Female Employment in the EMENA Region', Report prepared for the World Bank by Birks and Sinclair Ltd., Mountjoy Research Centre, Durham, 1991.

DaVanzo, J., and Lee, D.L.P., 'The Compatibility of Child Care with Market and Nonmarket Activities: Preliminary Evidence for Malaysia', in Buvinic, M., Lycette, M.A., and McGreevy, W.P., (eds.), *Women and Poverty in the Third World*, Baltimore: Johns Hopkins University Press, 1983, pp.62-91.

Le Grand, J., *The Strategy of Equality*, London: Unwin Hyman, 1982.

Killingsworth, M.R., and Heckman, J.J., 'Female Labor Supply: A Survey', in Ashenfelter, O., and Layard, P.R.G., *Handbook of Labour Economics*, Handbooks in Economics Series, No.5, Volumes 1 and 2, Amsterdam: North-Holland, 1986, pp.103-204.

Paoli, C., 'Women Workers and Maternity: Some Examples from Western Europe', *International Labour Review*, 121.1, 1982, pp. 1-16.

Papps, I., *For Love or Money: A Preliminary Economic Analysis of Marriage and the Family*, Hobart Paper No. 86, London: Institute of Economic Affairs, 1980.

Smith, J.P., and Ward, M., 'Women in the Labor Market and in the Family', *Journal of Economic Perspectives*, 3.1, 1989, pp. 9-23.

Townsend, P., and Davidson, N., (eds.), *Inequalities in Health*, Harmondsworth: Penguin, 1982.

Wilkinson, R., 'Socio-economic Factors in Mortality Differentials', M. Med. Sci. Thesis, University of Nottingham, 1976.

84

Notes

1   However, there is considerable evidence that the female labour force participation rate is consistently under-enumerated by conventional data collection methods.

2   For example, DaVanzo and Lee (1983) in a time budget study of Malaysian women found that working women had less leisure time than women who did not participate in the paid labour force.

3   See Killingsworth and Heckman (1986) for a survey of such studies.

4   It would be difficult to argue that many of these policies were justified to improve the allocation of resources. See Papps (1980) for further discussion of this point.

5   It is a standard result of economic theory that it is better, from the point of view of the recipients, to undertake redistribution by mean of income transfers rather than by subsidies on particular goods.

6   See Smith and Ward (1989) for an examination of this phenomenon in the US labour market.

7   See Townsend and Davidson (1982) for a summary of the evidence on the link between health status and socio-economic class in the UK.

8   See Le Grand (1982: Table 3.1) for some data on the relationship between medical services and socio-economic class which shows that the more affluent obtain more services when ill than do those who are less fortunate, although Le Grand himself does not place great emphasis on the importance of medical care for health. Wilkinson (1976) argues that diet is an important determinant of health and that diet is determined by income rather than by education.

9   Figures 1 and 2 are drawn excluding Turkey (which is a notable outlier) in order to obtain a scale which is large enough to demonstrate the pattern. However, all numerical calculations include Turkey where the relevant data are available.

10 The coefficient of correlation between the female labour force participation rate and life expectancy is 0.37 which is very low given that this index can take values between 0 and 1.

11 The coefficient of correlation for women is 0.71.

12 Relative life expectancy is measured as the ratio of female-to-male life expectancy; a similar definition is used for all other relative values.

13 The coefficient of correlation is 0.05.

14 The coefficient of correlation is 0.71.

15 Paoli (1982) is a notable exception although much else that is written under the auspices of the ILO ignores the point.

16 An implicit recognition of employers' unwillingness to employ women workers in such circumstances may be part of the reason for legislation aimed at ensuring equal pay and equal opportunities.

17 However, it would not increase the observed wage since the subsidy would make women willing to accept less from their employers. It is this effect which would tend to increase the level of employment.

18 See Birks *et al.* (1991) for a more detailed discussion of this point.

5

Women, Capitalism and Welfare

Joan Kennedy Taylor

Two things seem to have happened at once in the United States, and to a lesser extent, in Great Britain; women started having babies out of wedlock in large numbers, and an identifiable underclass emerged in slum neighbourhoods. These neighbourhoods were dirty and dangerous; their crime rates were high and their educational achievement and employment rates low; they seemed to be disintegrating.

Many of the people who live in these neighbourhoods live off government stipends and subsidies; many of them are children of people who were similarly supported and have known no other way of life. It is beginning to be feared that such neighbourhoods are self-perpetuating.

Single Mothers and Underclass Poverty

Are the phenomena of illegitimate births and of underclass poverty and deterioration related? American social scientist Charles Murray certainly thinks so. In a book review in the American journal, *Critical Review*,[1] he calls the proportion of births to single women 'the most important indicator of all, in my view, for what it says about the future of the inner city', and reports that (in the United States) 'the percentage of children born to single women in the inner city is somewhere in excess of 80 per cent in most urban areas'.

Extrapolation of statistical trendlines lead to paradoxical conclusions, but even if we don't follow them to those conclusions, they are scary. In 1982 it was reported in the United States that the National Advisory Council on Economic Opportunity had predicted that 'if the proportion of the poor in female-householder families were to continue to increase at the same rate as it did from 1967 to 1978, the poverty population would be composed solely of women and their children before the year 2000'.[2] And Charles Murray, in his paper entitled 'The Emerging British Underclass', first published in *The Sunday Times Magazine*,[3] and republished by the IEA Health and Welfare Unit in 1990, said that 'it is impossible to assume that the exponential curve in the trendline since 1970 will continue to steepen—if it were to do so, all British births would be illegitimate by the end of the century'.[4]

A March 22, 1991 editorial in *The Orange County (California) Register* cites the American Census Bureau, that 'children whose parents separate or divorce are twice as likely to fall into poverty as would have otherwise been the case'. Experts are finding that single mothers, however they got there, are a major part of the people on welfare, and also finding a correlation between the congregation in neighbourhoods of a particularly kind of single mother, the one who never married, and what has come to be known as the underclass.

Although these trends are occurring both in the United States and in the United Kingdom, there are differences as well as similarities between the two countries. What I have to say will primarily be drawn from the US; perhaps it will turn out that some of the general points I come to make will prove to be applicable at least in part to the UK as well.

Two attempted political solutions are suggested for this 'Problem of Poverty'. The solution labelled as liberal is to budget more money and benefits for those needing them, who have for over twenty years been told they are entitled to them. But unfortunately, American politicians have discovered that they can no longer ignore a federal budget deficit in the trillions—the voters will not allow it. And since each state is generally required to balance its budget each year, the 'solution' of devolving the care of the poor onto the states does not allow for much increase in budgets.

So there are conservative solutions that attempt to answer the problem by requirements and incentives. Congress passed a

Family Support Act in 1988 that tied eligibility for federal funds to states having 'workfare' programmes. These programmes were to include 7 per cent of employable people on welfare every month by 1991, and 20 per cent by 1995. At first, this meant required participation in unpaid government jobs for recipients 'able to work'. More recently, they have included a range of public and private jobs and job training. And states are instituting their own reforms. In February, 1991, the Governor of Wisconsin proposed that welfare recipients must either finish high school or get job training; welfare payments to unmarried teenage mothers should be capped, no matter how many children they had; and bonuses would be paid to those who marry. Other states were considering programmes ranging from child care for those finishing school to payments to recipients who surgically implant contraceptives to paying childbirth expenses for mothers putting their children up for adoption.

Caring for the Poor

The idea of caring for the poor originated in Western society in feudal times. At first, such care was the purview of the manor house and the church. When the feudal system began to break down and people formerly attached to the land began to move about, the first government statutes regarding the poor seem to have been primarily an attempt to enforce work norms. In 1349, the British Statute of Labourers made clear that private charity to the able-bodied was to be outlawed to achieve this purpose:

> Because that many valiant beggars, as long as they may live of begging, do refuse to labour, giving themselves to idleness and vice, and sometimes to theft and other abominations; none upon the said pain of imprisonment, shall under the colour of pity or alms, give anything to such, which may labour, or presume to favour them towards their desires, so that thereby they may be compelled to labour for their necessary living.[5]

In 1531, Parliament decreed that local officials should register the non-able-bodied poor on parish lists, and give them written permission to beg. Others were to be allowed some form of relief from local funds. Gertrude Himmelfarb describes 'the introduction of a national, legal, compulsory, public system of relief, the

first such in modern history', in *The Idea of Poverty*. 'The Eliza-
bethan poor laws', she writes,

> ... established the principles of the 'old poor law' as it later became
> known: the parish as the basic unit of administration, a compul-
> sory poor rate levied on householders by overseers appointed by
> the local justices (the overseers obliged to serve under penalty of
> a fine), and various types of relief for various kinds of needy—alms
> and almshouses for the aged and infirm, apprenticeship for
> children, and work for the able-bodied (and punishment or
> confinement for the 'sturdy beggar').[6]

In general the idea was both to offer relief to those who needed
it and to enforce work—for reasons of morality but also to keep
the poor from being too much of a drain on society. These
principles were brought to the American colonies, and when later
British legislation established workhouses, the United States
established them too.

There were differences. 'America', says Gertrude Himmelfarb,
'... took over the principles of the English poor laws but administered them in an atmosphere that was at the same time more
egalitarian and more intolerant of poverty than England'.[7]

With the Industrial Revolution, urban poverty and slums came
to the United States, followed by, in the late nineteenth century,
new ideas about the exploitation of workers. Poorhouses
remained in rural areas, but the cities were crowded with
working poor. Reformers who moved into poor neighbourhoods
in the settlement house movement (modeled on the founding of
England's Toynbee Hall in 1884) worked actively for social
legislation. If all factory work was exploitation of the worker by
the capitalist, then unless a benevolent government set limits to
the requirements of that work, it wasn't protecting its citizens.
In this context, what was ultimately a very destructive concept
arose, one which had a particularly punitive effect on women.
That was the concept of the *substandard*.

Regulation and legislation began to limit the ways in which
women could compete in the market-place, in the name of
protecting people against the substandard, whether it was in
housing, in wages, or in working conditions. Take housing as an
example.

Housing and the Poor

How do the poor find housing? In his review of *New Homeless and Old: Community and the Skid Row Hotel*, by Charles Hoch and Robert A. Slayton in *Critical Review*, Howard Husock compared the late nineteenth and early twentieth centuries with the 1980s.

> Using an array of social history sources—from city directories to narrative accounts of life in such hotels—they provide the means to understand the cheap hotel [single-room occupancy (SRO) lodgings] as a vital buffer between the poor and homelessness, a buffer whose decline—hastened in part, by purposeful demolition by public authorities—helped precipitate the rise in homelessness which became manifest in the 1980s. Hoch and Slayton use accounts of SRO history, particularly though not exclusively in Chicago, as the lens through which to see the larger issue of how housing for the poorest has been provided.... It was housing not only accepted but preferred, according to Hoch and Slayton, because it provided both privacy and some sense of community. Citing a 1964 study of the nation's best-known Skid Row—the Bowery in New York—they report that 'the most common phrases used by residents to describe their life-style and environment were positive ones, in particular that "no one bothers me" and that each person is "free to come and go"'.[8]

At the turn of the century, a private housing market was taking care of the huge influx of workers to the cities. The single-room occupancy lodgings varied from middle-class hotels with 'stationery and desks' to 'cage hotels' that had only a 'bed, mattress, quilt, chair, locker and light bulb' in a five-by-seven foot cubicle with limited toilet access and often only one shower for several hundred men. But a number of services, such as Turkish baths and trunk shops for storage, located near these hotels, and workers preferred them to the newly provided dormitory municipal shelters, because the cages had doors that locked.[9]

Reformers attacked the old SROs as substandard, and beginning in 1949, urban renewal wiped them out. And 'building code safety and amenity requirements' did not allow the market to replace them at any affordable cost. Husock tells us 'The ways in which traditional SRO tenants traded off comfort for savings simply became illegal'.[10] Society preferred to have them on the streets. (*Finally* there are moves to modify some US housing regulations to permit the building of modern SROs, or even to provide portable shelters that can be locked.)

But what specifically hurt women was when similar reforms were applied to rooming houses and the taking in of boarders. (Husock's article cites a 1920s Illinois Lodging House Register listing 1,139 rooming and lodging houses on Chicago's North Side, 92 per cent of which were owned by women.[11]) Robert Smuts, in a 1959 book, *Women and Work in America* (reprinted in paperback in 1971), says that, around the turn of the century, the 'most common way' that city women made money at home was by taking in boarders.

> Immigrant and low-income families were most likely to take in boarders.... Sometimes family and boarders lived together, two in a bed, six or eight in a room, and up to twenty or thirty in one small house or flat.[12]

By today's standards such crowding is unsanitary, but in earlier America, it was worth it for many families. Taking in boarders and other relatively unskilled work that women could do at home could make a family upwardly mobile. Nevertheless, the primary ways in which women could combine earning money with staying at home to raise children were gradually lessened or eliminated by 'protective' measures. Welfare or the dole were apparently considered more civilized than allowing such work to continue, since that was what was at the end of this policy line for poor women.

Working Mothers

First of all, the two-paycheque family is not a new phenomenon; it is merely new for the middle and upper classes. The majority of women have always worked, and, except on the farm, worked for money. The old saying of a poor community existing by 'taking in each other's washing', has some truth to it. Since US cities began to be filled with immigrants seeking work, when poor families were the majority of families, such families have traditionally remained stable when there were ways in which the mother of small children could remain at the centre of the home and still be a productive part of the economy. How could this be done? Besides taking in boarders, by sewing at home, participating in cottage industry at home (making cigars, for instance), or caring for children at home. And, yes, taking in laundry. All of these activities have gradually been curtailed or banned outright by government regulations in the United States.

As recently as 1989, when the American Department of Labor wanted to rescind a 1940 regulation against the manufacture of articles of women's clothing in the home, witnesses at a government hearing said the action would create 'sweatshops' and exploitation.

Regulators and the Market

Regulators really have a profound disdain for the market and for people's right to make choices. The assumption behind the reforms that took certain choices out of the market seems to be that if certain choices that are considered substandard are forbidden by law, better ones will emerge through the market. But that very often is not the case. So the reformers assume further, that if the market cannot rise to their standards, the government can do so, because it is not 'restrained' by the profit motive. But even in the face of government stipends and government services, we see ample evidence that people would still choose the substandard.

Today in the US we are witnessing the phenomenon of people who prefer to live out of shopping carts under bridges and in parks rather than go to public shelters. And recent immigrants, when they can, often temporarily find shelter for an entire family in one room, like the immigrant boarders of yesteryear. Such crowding is now, of course, totally illegal in the US, but some immigrants have found it preferable to going on the streets. Are we to say they are wrong?

When it comes to working conditions and wages, we see a similar story. The government, said *The New York Times* on March 12, 1989, estimated 'that hundreds of thousands of people are now working illegally in their homes', and the *Times* quoted a union representative as saying 'I have found sweatshops in

92

basements, garages, back porches, and kitchens.... Women are working 40 to 60 hours a week and ending up making $4.20 an hour'.

Child Labour

One of the most controversial issues today is the role of children in the 'substandard' labour market in late nineteenth and early twentieth century America. Children not only helped in industry in the home, such as cigar making, they frequently went out to work in factories. The definition of a child was different in a day when most children left school at the age of fourteen. But there were many children younger than that in American factories. Robert Smuts tells us that the revealed wisdom of the day was that, if at all possible, the mother should stay home and run the house.

> When a family was not supported by the father, the obligation to work fell on older sons, older daughters, younger sons, and younger daughters, in that order. The mother was usually the last to take a job.[13]

This was a period in which poor farm children were still routinely being bound out as apprentices by the courts. A 1989 article in the *Legal Studies Forum* gives this explanation.

> To a large extent, and without perhaps being fully aware of the implications of their own position, the reformers of charity defined someone's worth as the ability to survive economically; from such a definition it easily followed that the primary obligation of people was to be economically productive....

> Putting children to work and training them for work were fundamental principles both on the poor farm and in the mainstream of the reform movement.[14]

Thus there was, in Ms. Smith's words, agreement 'on the virtue of child labor'.[15] But later reformers saw nothing but evil, and again, exploitation, in productive work for children. I would like to offer another suggestion.

It is in the nature of human life that we produce our own livelihood. Compared to other mammals, children have a long period of infancy, during which they are cared for and educated by their parents. Isn't an important part of that education learning how to produce a livelihood? Shouldn't we welcome the idea of children learning to work by working for money? I suggest that what a society should be ashamed of is producing a generation of slum dwellers with little ability to form work habits, not of producing children who want to earn money too early and are willing to take low-paying jobs.

Educator John Holt tackled this question in a 1980 article attacking the role of schools in weakening the attachment to work.

> When we talk about young people's alienation from work, we must remember that we are talking about a problem that would not exist if we had not created it. The human animal is by its very nature not just an inquiring, thinking, dreaming, playing animal, but also a working animal. It is in our nature to want to shape the world around us, to make things and do things, and to want to do them as well as we can. We have only to watch little children at play to see how diligently and carefully they work at most of what they have chosen to do. We do not have to teach them to work, any more than we have to teach them to learn. But when, in school or even at home, we begin to train children to do what we want in order to get our rewards, we slowly destroy their capacity for pride and pleasure in work.[16]

But that's not the way expert thinking goes today. In June 1991, the Legislature of the State of New York voted to make New York's child-labour law one of the strictest in the United States. The new regulations, said The New York Times,[17] limited 'the number of hours youths can work while in school and prohibiting them from working past 10 p.m. on school nights without permission from their parents and teachers'. A shortage of workers has made many fast food restaurants that employ teenagers offer wages above the minimum wage. The Commissioner of Education said that higher wages make the jobs more appealing, 'and therefore make the restrictions more urgent.' A study reported in The New York Times in December, 1989, had found 22,508 children working nationally in violation of the Fair Labor Standards Act. Said The New York Times,

94

The children do not complain, nor do their parents; they like the extra money. Labor officials acknowledge that working in fast-food outlets or selling legitimate products door to door can help keep children away from drugs and other dangers as well as teach them the virtues of work.[18]

Still, New York toughened its laws on child labour, at the same time that experts in New York City were deploring the fact that 15 per cent of the city's population was on welfare and social policy experts were advocating compulsory workfare programmes to instill in members of the underclass some sort of ability to get up in the mornings and go to work regularly. In 1990, the Federal government accused the Salvation Army of exploiting the people it sheltered by giving them 'three hots and a cot' in exchange for working around the Salvation Army centres. The government said such people should be paid the minimum wage, a requirement the Salvation Army said might close the rehabilitation programmes, which have traditionally supported themselves without government aid.[19]

Welfare: A Women's Issue?

Periodically, feminists in the United States say that welfare is a women's issue. It *is* a women's issue, but that doesn't mean that the remedy is more government money or government programmes. As I've tried to indicate, a case can be made for the idea that it is government actions that have created many of the problems of people on welfare. For welfare mothers today, welfare is a psychological issue. I have suggested elsewhere[20] that, just as young women in the 1950s were convinced by the 'feminine mystique' to look on marriage and motherhood as the way to lives of their own, so young girls in American ghettoes today have a new version of the feminine mystique. They have so little to look forward to that they see motherhood supported by welfare as the only way to lives of their own—and they often 'marry' welfare to get it.

When Betty Friedan's book, *The Feminine Mystique*,[21] identified in 1963 that a generation of supposedly happy and fulfilled housewives had a 'problem that had no name', the problem of lack of a sense of identity and purpose, she was speaking to middle-class, educated women who by and large had the resources and the freedom of action to do something about it.

What was the situation of these housewives in the late fifties and early sixties? They had chosen early marriage because they saw no alternative. Early marriage was expected by society in general and their friends in particular. Young men, recently demobilised from World War II, wanted early marriage and didn't want their wives to work. Often families expected young women to live at home until marriage. Employers expected female employees to work until marriage and then quit; they did not expect a commitment to the work place or to a career from women, (except perhaps in the arts). So they had to face the obstacles a market society can put up in the face of change—the prejudice of employers, their own lack of skills (or rusty skills), the hostility of families unwilling to adjust to a partial loss of their services, and the reluctance of educational institutions to provide facilities for them.

What they had to change before they could challenge these obstacles was the attitude that had led them into their situation in the first place. They had to learn to value themselves as individuals, rather than in their roles as wives and mothers. Women all over the country made a difficult, strenuous, patient, and personal effort, in small groups. It was precisely the value of service to others, of thinking of oneself only (as Betty Friedan put it) as 'being Jimmy's mother or John's wife', that was questioned by women in this consciousness raising revolution.

Is there a parallel between those trapped housewives and the trapped inner-city mothers on welfare? Perhaps. First of all, we have to acknowledge that social trends are the result of individual choices, which in turn rest on assumptions about reality. These assumptions are reinforced by what one sees others in the community doing, particularly ones peers. In the summer of 1989, economist Elaine McCrate spoke at Radcliffe's Bunting Institute on teenage pregnancy, and, according to the summer issue of *Radcliffe News*,

> She disagreed with the conventional wisdom ... that teenage mothers, the majority of whom are poor, perpetuate their own poverty by becoming parents, discontinuing their schooling, and in

turn permanently damaging their opportunities for career growth and economic security. Inherent in this belief, said McCrate, is the assumption that economic opportunities exist for these young women.

... By analyzing women's wages, taking into account such factors as race, educational attainment, experience, tenure on the job, geographic region, union membership, and other factors, McCrate discovered that teenage mothers' educations contributed to only slight increases in earnings, and that this remained true even after considering the potential impact of teenage birth on the educational experience itself.

... If this is the case, then it follows that these young women have no reason or incentive to avoid early childbirth.[22]

Now, clearly, if you are the daughter of a mother who became pregnant in high school, if you know a number of girls your age or a little older who have started having babies and seem to find it rewarding, if you look at your school and know you aren't learning anything, and look at the earnings of your peers and see that the high school graduates and the non-graduates earn about the same salaries, there is little reason *not* to have a child. Similarly, young high school or college graduates after World War II were the daughters of non-working mothers, knew countless people of their generation who were marrying and having babies right after graduation, were getting a good education but not one that connected with opportunities in the job market, and saw few meaningful job opportunities that wouldn't just be a holding pattern until eventual marriage.

But in both cases, these environmental encouragements are only peripheral supports for a decision based on emotional needs. What's the emotional motive to make these decisions? The reason I say that these are feminist issues is that I think that in each case, the woman sees a closed society facing her, a society that requires risk-taking and the possibility of loneliness and failure in order to try to gain something. The decision to fulfil woman's biological function is a retreat from these unacceptable risks, that still seems to offer some much needed self-esteem. Now that the economic reasons for poor families to stay together have been shattered by government actions, and slum families have become fragmented, the literature is full of anecdotes of the girl who wants a baby 'to have something of my own', or 'to have someone to love me'. If most of the young men in the neighbourhood aren't working or seeking work (another characteristic of the underclass), she's not going to see a household with a man as stable. But welfare is stable, even though it is unsatisfactory. In the UK having a baby will even get her to the top of the list for housing of her own. When the decision to have a baby is made by default, so to speak, it is ultimately disappointing, and doesn't lead to the happy life the girl hopes for.

So if government restrictions have taken away from poor women the ability to make money at home while caring for their children; if they have at the same time, as experience both in the US and the UK indicates, produced a large number of young men so discouraged about regular work that they no longer look for it with any enthusiasm; if, further, government relief programmes do little but perpetuate the status quo, with little incentive to change it—what *is* the solution?

The Solution

First, to realize that government reforms won't work. The liberal and the conservative reforms alike have only succeeded in producing a miniature command economy. And the disintegration of the Soviet Union and of Eastern Europe have taught us that command economies can't work; a new and improved plan doesn't do the trick.

What is the alternative to a command economy? Privatization, and especially deregulation. If social policy makers could give up the old Marxist-influenced idea that work is somehow exploitation, and allow teenagers to work without permits and restrictions, allow women to earn money at home, allow people to choose the very cheap, even if it seems 'substandard' this would help. Older women, for instance, enjoy working in child care centres, but regulations in many states require formal training courses in order to be licensed. Why?

Second, one of the main results of government taking over in slum areas has been the downgrading or even destruction of groups. In this respect, the inner-city welfare mother is again like the fifties victim of the feminine mystique. In the fifties, housewives were isolated in their suburban homes from other women. In the slums today, they are similarly isolated. How can they undergo a revolution of consciousness, and start to take charge of their lives?

The strength of groups, including the family, has been eroded. In the nineteenth century, a network of mutual aid societies in the United States provided non-condescending help to their members, all of whom usually belonged to the same ethnic group. (In a special issue on welfare of *Critical Review*,[23] David Beito's article points out that many of these were in black neighbourhoods.) But there are non-governmental groups in the United States with useful programmes. Churches are building houses for the poor and even shopping malls; a number of organizations are counselling single mothers. A crusading Philadelphia school principal, Madeline Cartwright, wants to see a programme of 'mentor families' allowed to live in vacant houses in slum neighbourhoods and paid several thousand dollars a year to help troubled families with such elementary skills as budgeting, shopping, and housekeeping. A Los Angeles doctor started a similar programme called Adopt-a-Family, that recruits local stable families to give a family food, clothes, and especially advice for a year. This is the way women's liberation grew, only the skills those women needed then were how to write a résumé and how to apply to college when you'd been out of school for over ten years.

What about the power of advertising? Mothers Against Drunk Driving and its subsidiary, Students Against Drunk Driving has had enormous effect in the States with television advertisements against driving while drinking. The concept of a designated driver, almost unknown a few years ago, is credited to them. Might some non-profit group start a 'You Have a Future' campaign aimed at inner city teenage women, both those who are not mothers and those who are? Most of them do watch television. Each advert might give one piece of helpful information about job training, job placement, or a brief interview with someone who has an interesting and possible career, or, eventually, information about deregulation that has opened up an opportunity.

Can the disastrous unintended creation of underclasses be reversed? Big changes can occur in society through the power of ideas whose time has come. But it is ideas and the hope of choice that move people, not government programmes, however well intentioned.

Notes

1 Vol. 4, No. 4, p. 501.

2 Quoted in Barbara Ehrenreich and Karin Stallard, 'The Nouveau Poor', *Ms.*, July/August 1982.

3 26 November 1989.

4 London: IEA Health and Welfare Unit, 1990, p. 23.

5 Quoted in Piven, Frances Fox, and Richard A. Cloward, *Regulating the Poor: The Functions of Public Welfare*, New York: Pantheon, 1971.

6 New York: Alfred A. Knopf, 1984, p. 25.

7 *Ibid.*, p. 17.

8 Howard Husock, 'The Roots of Homelessness', *Critical Review*, Vol. 4, No. 4, pp. 507-8.

9 Husock, *op. cit.*, pp. 509-10.

10 Husock, *op. cit.*, p. 512.

11 Husock, *op. cit.*, p. 509.

12 New York: Schocken Books, 1971, p. 15-16.

13 Smuts, *op. cit.*, p. 43.

14 Charlene L. Smith, 'Children on Kansas Poor Farms: 1860-1900', *Legal Studies Forum*, Vol. 13, No. 3., p. 258.

15 Smith, *op, cit.*, p. 259.

16 John Holt, 'Growing Up Engaged', *Psychology Today*, July 1980, p. 23.

17 Sam Howe Verhovek, 'New Limits Set on Job Hours for Students', *The New York Times*, 29 June, 1991.

18 Peter T. Kilborn, 'Playing Games With Labor Laws: When Work Fills a Child's Hours', *The New York Times*, 10 December, 1989.

19 Anthony DePalma, 'Salvation Army is Told to Pay Minimum Wage', *The New York Times*, 16 September, 1990.

20 Joan Kennedy Taylor, 'The Welfare Mystique', *Inquiry*, November 1982, pp. 10-13.

21 New York: W.W. Norton & Company, Inc., 1963.

22 Heather Clark, 'Teenage Pregnancy: Economic Irrationality or Logical Choice?', *Radcliffe News*, Summer 1989, pp. 4-5.

23 Vol. 4, No. 4, pp. 709-36.

6

Preferential Treatment of Women in Employment

Wendy McElroy

One of the political issues that the 1990s will inherit from the '80s is the preferential treatment of women in employment. This treatment is considered necessary in order to afford women equal access to jobs and other opportunities from which they have been excluded for decades... sometimes for centuries. The preferential policies cover a wide spectrum of concerns, from properly conducted job recruitment to pregnancy leave to adequate advancement for women. The literature surrounding such policies is immense.

But perhaps a more interesting approach to the preferential treatment of women is to examine the fundamental arguments and principles underlying all policies of preference for women. A good question to start with is: where have these policies come from? What is the proximate cause of our current laws on the subject?

During the social turbulence of the 1960s and '70s in the United States, radical reformers voiced a clear demand: discrimination must end! People must not be slotted according to sex, race, or religion. Their call for equality had the ring of justice and their cause quickly gained popularity. After all, equal justice before the law and equal access to political power is a well entrenched American ideal.

But this was not the ideal being promoted. The reformers were introducing a comparatively new sense of equality into the American arena—that of social equality. They demanded far more than the removal of legal barriers based on sex; they pressed for equal access to certain basic necessities, such as housing and education. Only by assuring basic needs to disadvantaged people, it was argued, could these victims compete on an equal footing with advantaged people—in this case, with white males. In essence, the reformers proposed nothing less than a new social order based on a primitive form of socioeconomic equality.

Where did women stand in this new social order? Virtually no one denied that women had endured legal discrimination for centuries. Although these barriers had been largely removed, it was argued that the effects of such a longstanding injustice were still evident and having an impact on present generations. The lingering injustice was especially apparent in the market-place, which continued to undervalue woman's labour and to exploit her secondary status in society. Correcting this situation required much more than the repeal of discriminatory laws; it required the institution of laws and policies that actively preferred women. Only by being preferred could women be equal. Mary C. Thornberry, in her essay 'Affirmative Action: History of An Attempt to Realise Greater Equality', explained this necessity:

> Broadly speaking, affirmative action measures include a whole range of special steps designed to overcome the consequences of past and present discrimination. These include compensatory and remedial training, validations of tests and criteria for jobs or university admission, the development by employers of recruiting procedures aimed at women and minorities as well as other qualified applicants, provision of child-care centers and remedial programs to remove handicaps in employment, and related measures to help the disadvantaged realize their potential... In order to overcome the effects of past practices which resulted in discrimination, companies must now seek out those who were formerly ignored.[1]

'Institutional Discrimination'

It was during the 1960s that a new phrase came into popular use: the phrase was 'institutional discrimination'. This has been defined as: 'those institutional arrangements whereby certain categories of people are either excluded from or disadvantaged in the distribution of power'. Institutional discrimination was distinguished from personal prejudice. For example, a company with no bias against women might confine its recruitment search or hiring to its local community, in which there simply are no qualified women. This effectively prevents a woman from competing for the position. Thus, from such an innocent motive as civic pride, the company could be guilty of institutional discrimination. The key to this discrimination is not the intention of the company, but how it apportioned its power and opportunities—in terms of private property, social good, might makes right, equality, or some other standard? To advocates of preference only one method of apportionment—that of social equality—is considered justified.

Even for the well-intentioned employer, the price of institutional discrimination can be very high. Although preferential policies are not always mandated by law, they have been well established through administrative regulations and judicial rulings. Most states have Fair Employment Practice Laws that allow defendants to file discrimination charges.

Myra K. Wolfgang, speaking as a representative of the Michigan Women's Commission, well expressed the spirit of these Employment Laws:

> We, who want equal opportunities, equal pay for equal work and equal status for women, know that frequently we obtain real equality through a difference in treatment, rather than identity in treatment.[2]

Preferential Policies

How does this the theory of preferential policies impact upon the real world? In 1980, after losing a discrimination suit, the Ford Motor Company was forced to spend $13 million in back pay to women and minorities. In 1983, the General Motors Company faced a similar situation; it agreed to pay $42.5 million, largely toward the education and training of women and minorities.

In such suits, the attorney fees alone have encouraged employers to impose a safe quota system upon themselves. In a sex discrimination case against the University of Minnesota, for example, the attorney fees amounted to $1,475,000. To no one's

104

surprise, the successful plaintiff abandoned the academic life to become a lawyer. Since US law requires an unsuccessful defendant to pay *all* legal fees as well as any of several possible awards of money, employers have instituted preferential policies as a means of self-defense.

Thus, the business world has accepted preferential policies in the recruitment, employment and promotion of women in order to ensure that women are 'adequately' represented. The business world is confronted with a *de facto* quota system that requires employers to prefer women over men in order to prove that they are treating women the same as men.

This is a contradiction in terms. It flies blatantly in the face of the very ideal it is said to promote: equality. How did the ideal of an equal and just society become tied to this contradiction? Only an analysis and a critique of the fundamental arguments for the preference of women can shed light on this dilemma.

Social Planning

Before dealing directly with the arguments, however, it is necessary to address a related issue: that of statistical analysis. Social planning has been called the step-child of statistical analysis. The 'technology of social measurement' has been, perhaps, the most powerful weapon used by advocates of preference. Indeed, social indicators have been used as the standard to identify whether or not institutional discrimination exists in any particular situation. R.A. Bauer, in his work *Social Indicators* has defined these tools as:

> Statistical indexes by which demographers, population analysts, and social policy analysts estimate the state-of-being of a given population, at a given time, with respect to a particular set of characteristics previously determined (or thought) to be relevant to the state-of-being in question.[3]

This scientific definition—as confusing as it is—masks the immense problems facing anyone who attempts to measure such amorphous factors as opportunity, access and power. Indeed, many critics believe it is impossible to measure qualitative, as opposed to quantitative, differences.

The scientific definition also masks the crucial fact that *all* social scientists have biases or agendas that influence the objectivity of their statistics. As Howard Sherman explains:

> No social scientist is unbiased; all come from a particular social environment, and all have tentative conclusions (conscious or unconscious) on any issue they are investigating... Moreover, a social science that presented no conclusions would be useless. Imagine an engineer who tells us there are ten different ways to build the bridge we are considering, but refuses to tell us which he believes best under the circumstances.[4]

The problems of statistical analysis are well documented. Statistics attempt to measure elusive and vague factors such as opportunity; they generalize from particulars; and they contain the assumptions of the analysts. Moreover, statistics do not bring a context or a perspective to the raw data. For example, statistics revealing that women's wages rose after a piece of legislation do not indicate if the wages were rising before the legislation; nor do they offer a sense of cause and effect. Moreover, by the time statistics are accumulated, processed and converted into policy they may well be out-of-date.

Nevertheless, social planners use statistical analysis as though it were fully packaged knowledge... as though it were value-free. Backed by truckloads of statistics, they propose a radical solution which has been dressed up in an old ideal: equality. Translating their policies into the real world, they propose to regulate attitudes and behaviour—especially of the business community—so that all people have equal power in society. Equal opportunity for the disadvantaged is to be mandated, if not by law then by the threat of court action.

Arguments to Justify Preferential Treatment

In general, three arguments are used to justify the preferential treatment of women in employment. They are: (1) utilitarian or social good arguments; (2) arguments for compensatory justice, usually based on historical injustice; and (3) arguments for the ideal of equality.

The Utilitarian Argument

First, the utilitarian argument: this position states that society will be enriched by preferring women and allowing them to achieve equality.

There are several ways to criticise this argument. You could observe that utilitarian or pragmatic considerations tend to blow in the wind of circumstance; they change with each freshly elected administration, with every economic shift, and with many world events such as the declaration of war. To base the ideal of equality on the argument for utility is to lay a foundation of sand.

As well, you could speculate on the long term consequences to society of using a quota system rather than individual as the standard by which to allocate jobs and wealth. Preferential policies inevitably drive a wedge between individual worth and economic success. It is difficult to understand how this wedge enriches society.

But another critique of the utilitarian argument strikes more at the heart of preferential policies. It examines, in human terms, the costs and risks of forcing employers to prefer women simply because they are women. One cost is that those groups who are being discriminated against—in this case men—will be understandably resentful and they will translate their resentment into a heightened sexism. Instead of being overt, the new sexism will be subtle and covert. It will be less open to remedy through education and persuasion.

The effect on preferential policies on women could be equally devastating. In rushing to appear unbiased, employers will tend to promote women prematurely into jobs they are not prepared to handle; or they will promote women into whatever vacancies occur within the company, whether or not the women have the necessary background. When these women fail or perform in a mediocre manner, it will be seen as confirmation that women cannot handle high level positions.

And what of the women who succeed on nothing but their own merit and hard work? A *de facto* quota system preferring women will stigmatise every single women in the work force as inferior. In years past, it was assumed that women succeeded in business by sleeping with the boss; now it will be assumed that they succeed by virtue of political privilege. The woman who achieves excellence on her own will never receive the recognition she richly deserves.

In essence, preferential policies will increase the very prejudice (sexism) that it seeks to eliminate at the expense of the very group (women) that it seeks to benefit. This is the cost. And it contradicts a major assumption underlying the utilitarian approach: namely, that wealth and power can simply be transferred from one group to another. Advocates of preference assume that the transfer of wealth and power is a zero-sum game. The contrary is true. It is quite possible and, indeed, probable that everyone will lose. This is the risk.

But even discounting the above objections, it is difficult to imagine how the utilitarian argument for preference lives up to its own standards. Namely, can it be implemented? The question becomes: is it possible to control a massively complex and ever shifting set of social interactions? After all, people and society respond in unpredictable ways. The black economist Thomas Sowell has observed:

> Those who initiate preferential policies cannot sufficiently control the reactions of either preferred or non-preferred groups to ensure that such policies will have the desired effect... in the desired direction.[5]

Consider just one aspect of what would be required to regulate the fairness of employment: consider the vast and constant flow of knowledge that effective control would require. And, of course, a necessary context for this knowledge would be the assumption that you know what a non-discriminatory world looks like. Only with reference to this ideal can you tell when a situation is deviating from it; that is, when a situation constitutes discrimination. Advocates of preference tend to assume that non-discrimination would result in an employment pattern that accurately reflects the overall ratio of men to women. With this pattern in mind, you could simply look for deviations. But when does a deviation constitute discrimination? This requires further knowledge. For the deviation might result from such innocent factors as the age spread of a given community, or its geography.

The unvarnished truth is that human beings are diverse and disparity does not mean inequity. Any particular disparity may well be accidental or be caused by something unrelated. Of course, such disparities could be judged on a case-by-case basis, but this would involve such a bureaucratic nightmare that no-one suggests this alternative. The attitude seems to be: better the innocent should suffer than the guilty should go free. This attitude is embodied in the fact that companies who are sued must prove that no discrimination occurred: they are no longer innocent until proven guilty.

Compensatory Justice

The second argument advanced by advocates of preference is an appeal for compensatory justice. In law, this principle claims that anyone causing an injury to an innocent person must rectify the damage. The innocent party must receive compensation. Advocates of preference go one step further: they claim that the descendants of those injured must receive compensation as well. After all, it is argued, the descendants are still living with the consequences of centuries of discrimination. For example, the socio-economic status forced upon their mothers may have deprived them of a university education. This is an argument for righting historical wrongs.

Objections to 'the state as remedial historian' argument are myriad. One of the more basic ones is whether or not it is possible to rectify past injustices when the injured parties are dead. For the sake of argument, however, I am also granting several assumptions, such as the validity of the historical injustice under discussion, and the accuracy of the assessment of the wrong.

Instead, my objections to the use of preferential policies to correct historical wrongs fall into two categories: (1) I contend that the people receiving the benefits are not victims, and, (2) I contend that the people forced to provide the compensation have done no wrong.

Overwhelmingly, the women who receive the benefits of preferential policies are not the same women who suffered the centuries of injustice. The simple fact of human mortality assures this point. In essence, it is impossible to rewrite human history.

But, advocates of preference argue, the present generation of women still suffer from the shadow of history. For example, it is claimed that the 'under-representation' of women in the medical profession bears a direct relationship to the original injustice of barring them from this field. Thus, the heirs (at least, the female heirs) of victimised women have a valid claim to compensation.

This carries the theory of compensatory justice far beyond conventional legal practice. Even the path-breaking compensation granted to victims of the Holocaust did not encompass payments to future generations. Thus, the compensation embodied in preferential policies is open-ended with no possible limit to the amount owed by the guilty party. This flies in the face of legal theory, which demands a clear definition of punishment and payment.

To demand compensation for the grandchildren of victims is to confuse a justifiable sense of compassion with a legal claim. Present generations are undoubtedly influenced by many things that happened to their ancestors. But this is a matter of causality, not morality. The class into which you are born—whether defined by sex, race or social status—is an accident of nature. Even John Rawls—an advocate of distributive justice—concedes:

> The natural distribution is neither just nor unjust; nor is it unjust that persons are born into society at some particular position. These are simply natural facts.[6]

Rawls goes on: 'What is just and unjust is the way that institutions deal with these facts.'[7]

The questions remain: if there is no injustice, how can there be a legal claim for compensation? If the natural distribution is neither just nor unjust, what happens to the moral underpinning of socio-economic equality?

There is an interesting question that bears on this moral underpinning. Indeed, it can be used as a litmus test of whether or not advocates of preference are sincere about righting past history. The question is: what of the women of privilege? Are women from the Rockefeller family, for instance, to be given preferential treatment along with the working women allegedly exploited by them? If compensation is truly the goal, then women who have benefited from the history of oppression should be placed at a disadvantage rather than being preferred. The fact that such a policy has not been suggested sheds doubt on the much trumpeted goal of fighting for the underdog. At this point, the advocate of preference begins to look like just another advocate of government control and the redistribution of wealth.

My second objection to the argument for compensatory justice concerns the people who are forced to pay the compensation. (By the word 'pay', I refer not only to taxpayers, but to those men who are discriminated against and those business people who must submit to government regulation). My objection is fundamental: I do not believe guilt can be inherited. Herbert Deane in *Justice—Compensatory and Distributive* states this position well:

> Present members of the society are being asked to assume the responsibility not only for unjust acts in the present of the recent past in which they may have had no share, but also for acts of discrimination which were performed, long before they were born, and when, indeed their fathers and grandfathers may not have been Americans at all, but may have been suffering persecution and discrimination, for example, in Eastern Europe. We are, in other words, asked to accept the principle of collective guilt that is at least in part inherited from some of the ancestors of some contemporary Americans.[8]

Further, I do not believe that 'classes' of people—such as men—can be held guilty for actions in which they had no part as individuals. The strange compensation demanded by advocates of preference seems to violate a common sense notion of fairness. It requires certain people (men) to be legally disadvantaged in the name of equality. But questions of justice remain: can you morally deny equal opportunity to some members of society in order to give it to others? Or is this a contradiction in terms?

Perhaps the best overall critique of the argument for compensatory justice has been rendered by Thomas Sowell in his book *Preferential Policies: An International Perspective*:

111

Given the mortality of human beings, often the only compensation
for historic wrongs that is within the scope of our knowledge and
control is purely symbolic compensation—taking from individuals
who inflicted no harm and giving to individuals who suffered
none.[9]

The Ideal of Equality

The third argument commonly advanced for the preferential
treatment of women is an appeal to the ideal of equality. But
equality is an ambiguous word. People who use the word
'equality' frequently mean different and contrary things by it. To
some, any difference at all between human beings—social,
physical, economic, etc. constitutes an inequality. Others contend
that such differences are natural or even healthy. They might
assess the situation as being 'different or separate, but equal'.
Two examples of humans being different but equal are the
differences between those with brown and blue eyes, or those
with white and black skins. A difference becomes an inequality
only when a normative judgement is attached. Thus, if I say
'people with blue eyes are superior', then having brown eyes
ceases to be a difference and becomes an inequality.

The salient question for any definition of equality is: when
does a difference become an inequality? Traditionally, American
society has considered differences before the law or in access to
political power to be inequalities. This definition focuses on the
rights of the individual with regard to the state and says: 'every
individual should be free to pursue happiness, wealth and well-
being to the extent of his or her abilities to do so.'

Advocates of preference have a different definition of equality.
Even in the absence of legal or political barriers, they consider
any difference in the access of groups or classes to wealth and
power to constitute an inequality. This definition focuses on the
rights of certain classes (women or employees) as they relate to
other classes (men or employers). Their concept of equality is
based on socio-economics and class theory; it seeks to redistrib-
ute the wealth and power of society, usually through imposing
state control on erring individuals.

Thus, the definition of equality used by advocates of preference bears no resemblance to that used by advocates of individual rights. Indeed, they are incompatible on several points.

First, a preferential view of equality divides society into classes rather than viewing it as a collection of individuals. Discrimination and inequality exist only in the context of comparing one class with another. No distinction is made between innocent or guilty individuals—privileged or victimised women—because people are innocent or guilty by virtue of the class to which they belong. Lee Nisbet, in 'Affirmative Action—a Liberal Program?' asserts:

> We find here no concern for the individual. What the person *did* as a person is irrelevant. His gender and race in some mysterious way renders him guilty of offenses and deserving of admittedly unfair treatment. It hardly needs to be said that such proposals are neither liberal nor intelligent much less morally intelligible.[10]

Moreover, preferential policies reverse the traditional American safeguard of liberty—the protection of the rights of the individual against intrusion by the state. Instead, the state becomes the arbiter of justice in the conflicts between two classes of society. Perhaps this is a consequence of the belief that the law should function as a remedial historian and as a social analyst. This is in stark contrast to the established view of law—to protect individuals and property from violence. Now the purview of law has been expanded to include such acts, or non-acts, as refusing to hire someone. In essence, the law is used to impose morality rather than to enforce the peace.

The preferential treatment of women in employment is an attempt to destroy the free-market system. Preferential policies constitute an unprecedented government intrusion into the most basic of business decisions, i.e. who to hire and promote. It is an involvement which constitutes control. This is one small step away from the state control of privately owned business—which is to say, fascism.

Discrimination and the Free Market

The final irony is that the surest safeguard against discrimination is the very mechanism that is being destroyed: the free market.

Historically, the free market has tended to eliminate discrimination simply because it costs money. Discrimination reduces the pool of talent from which employees can be drawn; it alienates customers, on whose patronage companies live or die; and it lowers the efficiency of production since trained employees will not put up with discrimination, but will seek advancement elsewhere. Thus, the free market—in pursuit of profit—has tended to advance individual talent, regardless of sex or race.

But what of the state? Consider the case of racial discrimination in the American South. The civil rights movement arose in protest when an elderly black women was arrested for sitting in the front of a bus in Montgomery, Alabama. What role did the bus company play in this drama? Jim Crow laws—laws discriminating against blacks—had been part of Southern history for decades. Many bus companies refused to enforce them. For some companies, this may have been a moral stand; more likely, the bus companies simply did not wish to alienate black customers by forcing them to sit in the back. The streetcar company in Montgomery was among those who refused to discriminate. It reasoned: 'a customer is a customer'. Only when streetcar conductors were arrested for non-discrimination did the bus companies comply with the law.

The market-place is not less prejudiced than the community in which it operates. But it does function along different principles; it is there to make a profit. Thus, the free market—which is colour and sex blind to the source of its income—is a great leveller of prejudice.

The preferential treatment of women in employment is nothing less than a frontal attack on the rights of the individual and the free market. The demand for socio-economic equality runs against an ingrained sense of fairness: it runs against the sense that every individual has the right to the fruit of whatever talent or resource he or she possesses. Preferential policies can be likened to the shackling of the best runners at the beginning of a race so that no one can excel. It is not clear how such a policy can advance the well-being of society.

114

Notes

1   *Elusive Equality: Liberalism, Affirmative Action and Social Change in America*, Port Washington, N.Y.: Associated Faculty Press, 1983, pp. 50-1.

2   *America's Working Women: A Documentary History—1600 to the Present*, N.Y.: Vintage Books, 1976, p. 378.

3   Cambridge, Mass.: M.I.T. Press, 1966, p. 93.

4   *Radical Political Economy: Capitalism and Socialism from a Marxist-Humanist Perspective*, N.Y.: Basic Books, 1972, p. 6.

5   *Preferential Policies: An International Perspective*, N.Y.: William Morrow & Co., 1990, p. 124.

6   *A Theory of Justice*, Cambridge, Mass.: Harvard University Press, 1971, p. 102.

7   *Ibid.*

8   Columbia University Press, 1974, pp. 13-14.

9   N.Y.: William Morrow & Co., 1990, p. 160.

10 Barry R. Gross (ed.), *Reverse Discrimination*, Buffalo, N.Y.: Prometheus Books, 1977, p. 142.

Recent Health and Welfare Unit Publications

The Spirit of Democratic Capitalism

Feb. 1991, £12.95. 463pp. ISBN 0-8191-7823-3

PROFESSOR MICHAEL NOVAK

'Michael Novak . . . has done us a service in illuminating where the fault lines between right and left now lie.'   Will Hutton, *Guardian*

'Mr Major . . . might seek inspiration from *The Spirit of Democratic Capitalism* . . . There is much to be gained from a skip through.'
                    Joe Rogaly, *Financial Times*

Empowering the Elderly

May 1991, £6.95. 50pp. ISBN 0-255 36268-4

WILLIAM LAING

'Vulnerable and dependent people are not well served by monopolies which make discretionary decisions on their behalf', according to economist William Laing.

Is British Food Bad for You?

June 1991, £4.95. 36pp. ISBN 0-255 36267-6

PROFESSOR VINCENT MARKS

'A leading nutritionist makes a scathing attack on "food terrorists" who spread unscientific scare stories about so-called health foods.'
                    Independent

'Fad eating is the greatest food health risk in Britain . . . warns leading biochemist.'   *London Evening Standard*

Saving Lives

Sept. 1991, £5.95. 34pp. ISBN 0-255 36269-2

P. BASKETT, M. IRVING, B. MCKIBBIN & R. MURLEY

'More than 1,000 people die every year in Britain because of the failure of accident and emergency services, according to a report published today.'   *The Times*

The Moral Foundations of Market Institutions

Feb. 1992, £7.95. 156pp. ISBN 0-255 36271-4

JOHN GRAY

'one of the most intelligent and sophisticated contributions to conservative
philosophy.'   *The Times*

'this powerful tract ... is persuasive.'   *Financial Times*

Empowering the Parents

Sept. 1991, £6.95. 90pp. ISBN 0-255 36270-6

A. FLEW, M. SELDON, J. LE GRAND, D. ROBINSON
& R. CARR-HILL

'Good teachers have to be set free from the dead weight of politicians
and town hall bureaucrats, says the Institute of Economic Affairs.'
                                                              Liverpool Daily Post

Working Class Patients and the Medical Establishment

1985, £9.95. 211pp. Hardback. ISBN 0-85117-263-6

DAVID G. GREEN

'a unique study of the development of the relationship between
producers and consumers of primary medical care in the hundred years
up to the creation of the National Health Service ... a well documented
historical study.'   *Political Quarterly*

'a fascinating analysis of the actual workings of medicine under the
friendly societies ... Market competition actually served the needs of the
people well.'   *New Society*

'all important, if controversial, contribution.'   *Sociology*

Citizenship and Rights in Thatcher's Britain: Two Views

June 1990, £3.95. ISBN 0-255 36261-7

PROFESSOR RAYMOND PLANT, PROFESSOR NORMAN BARRY

Two leading political theorists describe and discuss the rights and
obligations of citizenship, Professor Plant arguing from a socialist
standpoint and Professor Barry from a classical-liberal perspective.